THE APPROPRIATE PLACEMENT SCHOOL:

A Sophisticated Nongraded Curriculum

THE
APPROPRIATE
PLACEMENT
SCHOOL:

A Sophisticated Nongraded Curriculum

B. FRANK BROWN *artley* , *1917-*

Parker Publishing Company, Inc., West Nyack, N. Y.

© 1965 BY

PARKER PUBLISHING COMPANY, INC.

WEST NYACK, NEW YORK

LIBRARY OF CONGRESS
CATALOG CARD NUMBER: 65-25810

Sixth printing . . . . September, 1968

PRINTED IN THE UNITED STATES OF AMERICA

04388—B&P

To
CHARLES R. KELLER
impassioned advocate of quality
in the public schools

PREFACE

The idea of an Appropriate Placement school with a multi-phased curriculum originated under unusual and unexpected circumstances. In May of 1963, the Panel for Educational Research and Development of the President's Science Advisory Committee commissioned me to organize and direct a conference of the nation's leaders in the nongraded school movement. The purpose of this educational venture was to determine the effectiveness of the nongraded design as a better model for educating that portion of the school population known as the "difficult thirty percent." The impulse behind the symposium was the new national concern for the dropout, the deprived, and the segregated.

The colloquy was held at the Massachusetts Institute of Technology and underwritten by funds from the White House budget. Present at the conference were the nation's leading university professors and educational leaders of the nongraded school movement. The list of participants included the following:

Jerrold R. Zacharias
Professor of Physics
Massachusetts Institute
of Technology

David Street
Sociology Department
University of Chicago
Chicago, Illinois

Maurie Hillson
Professor of Education
Bucknell University
Lewisburg, Pennsylvania

Robert M. Finley
Superintendent
Barrington Public Schools
Barrington, Illinois

James Lindsey
Principal
Grand Oaks School
Citrus Heights, California

George Peterson
Principal
Armstrong High School
Richmond, Virginia

Lore Rasmussen
Mathematics Laboratory
Miquon School
Miquon, Pennsylvania

B. Frank Brown
Principal
Melbourne High School
Melbourne, Florida

John I. Goodlad
Professor and Director
University Elementary School
University of California at
Los Angeles

Stephen White
Assistant to the President
Educational Services, Inc.
Watertown, Massachusetts

Joseph Turner
Office of Science &
Technology
Executive Office of the
President
Washington, D. C.

Myrtle Sullivan
Director of Counselors
Middletown High School
Middletown, Rhode Island

Lucille Thimblin
Principal
Southbridge Schools
Southbridge, Massachusetts

Warren W. Hamilton
Superintendent
Yellow Springs Schools
Yellow Springs, Ohio

Jerome H. Gilbert
Principal
Nikola Tesla Elementary
School
Chicago, Illinois

After two days of deliberation and debate, the conferees concluded that the nation's elementary and secondary schools are far too cautious to embark upon a truly exotic nongraded program. They concluded that the major roadblock to universal acceptance of the nongraded process is the lack of an orderly curriculum scheme to replace the graded organization. The major recommendation of the conference urged that a massive effort be made to develop a new educational blueprint which would accommodate and encourage continuous progress through school.

Spurred on by the ideas and notions generated at this important meeting, I have spent the past year working on a new curriculum model for nongraded schools. The search for new patterns carried me over a hundred thousand miles as I visited nongraded schools scattered from Massachusetts to Hawaii and from Mexico to Canada.

This book is a report on the dialogues of the M.I.T. conference and the subsequent discovery of a new stratagem for nongrading schools.

INTRODUCTION

A Vivid Glimpse of the Future [1]

What is so deeply important about abolishing grade levels in a school is that the nongraded system forces a complete re-evaluation of what one is trying to accomplish in the educational enterprise. It is not that a Procrustean system of grouping students according to their "year" is abolished, but that there is erected in its place something new and challenging and full of promise—a "multiphased curriculum." The Melbourne experiment in multiphased curricula is so daring and so general in its applicability that it earns the right to special attention for the glimpse it gives of the future.

"Nongrading" comes to terms with the obvious fact of vari-

---

[1] Professor Jerome Bruner's original impression of the nongraded school appeared in the January 18, 1963, issue of the *Saturday Review*. We gratefully acknowledge the permission of the *Saturday Review* to reprint this revised version of the original article. The revision was suggested by Dr. Bruner following a visit to Melbourne High School.

ability. Some students can go faster than their age-mates—
phenomenally faster, whether because of capacity or the
fortune of background. If one demands a standard amount of
work from all in any given grade, may we not be robbing the
student of the opportunity of learning and using his own pace?
Some will inevitably feel a sense of failure, however hard
they try, while others will squirm their way through a year of
unchallenged freedom. If a student can do college work in
mathematics or history in his freshman year in high school, let
him take Advanced Placement courses in those subjects from
the beginning right to his last year. And if another student
needs extra remedial work in mathematics in freshman year,
let him not be dumped into a regular or even a "slow" algebra
course to do his best—ending, likely, by memorizing matter
that makes no sense to him. Give him a course in the fundamentals he will need before launching him into algebra. These
are the kinds of considerations that have led to the decision
to "ungrade" schools. The idea is to eliminate the deadening
effects of a graded system (where failure is punished by having
to repeat the same work over).

School grading is simply a poor piece of technology for using
the resources of a school, one that has to be removed if the next
step is to be taken. It is like nothing so much as the replace-
ment of the top hitch by the horse collar during the medieval
period. Up to the introduction of the horse collar, the weight
to be hauled was attached to the top of a yoke by a strap that
passed over the horse's back. When the horse pulled, the yoke
pressed against his windpipe in a self-choking manner. The
innovation was a simple one: pass the strap under the horse's
body and attach it to the lower part of the collar. With thrust,
the collar would press against the horse's strong neck and
shoulders. He could then "put his back into it."

In the graded school, the eager student, pressed against the
system, has found himself stifled by the requirements of his

grade. Soon he regulates his thrust to suit the system. What often results is boredom for the swift, bewilderment for the slow, and a general surrender of intellectual aspirations to what teacher wanted.

In the multiphased school, courses have been reorganized into a system of "phases" that reflect not the grade in which they are taught, but the student's ability to grasp the subject and his willingness to throw his weight into the task. Phase 1 is the remedial section and it is designed for students who need special assistance in small classes. When a student feels ready to try something more advanced, he is encouraged to set forth to the next "phase." His willingness is a major criterion. Phase 2 is for students who need more emphasis on the basic skills of a subject. Phase 3 is for those who are ready to have a go at the major substance of the curriculum in the field. Phase 4 is the subject in depth and with concentration. Phase 5 is independent study for the exceptional student willing to assume responsibility for his own learning and ready to use all available resources in doing so. He is supervised by a teacher with whom (as in any tutorial system) the student makes an appointment when he has finished a stint of work. The phase system operates in four basic intellectual disciplines: mathematics, science, English, and history. They are the core of the process.

Virtually every one of the major curriculum efforts of the last decade has been incorporated and fitted to the needs of Melbourne's multiphased school—the Physical Science Study Committee course, the Chemical Bond course, the Biological Sciences Curriculum Study, several experimental mathematics programs, and some homegrown innovations in social studies and humanities. These courses can and are being adapted to different phase levels. There is no reason why the new curricula cannot be adapted to this broader use more generally.

But the realignment of the students on the basis of achievement changed course content in the nongraded school in subtle ways. The school perforce resorts to a much wider range of materials than those used in the graded school. Standard textbooks aimed at a grade level are inappropriate and have been abolished. A multiplicity of materials has replaced the rigid text. But there is more to it than that, something in the system that seems to challenge students to reach. Brown suggests it: "Motion itself is not the cure for monotony in the schools; liveliness of image is the key. The flexibility of the nongraded structure gives a new image to both the learning process and the educational establishment." The new "image" has the effect of making the student decide his pace, whether to get into a next phase or to undertake independent studies.

There are many little things in the multiphased curriculum that make up the image of mobility, things that individually are shrewd but in aggregate make educational wisdom. For one thing, a nongraded school is likely to boast that it has a library which is larger than its gymnasium. For another, the student who is engaged in independent studies or who is in pursuit of some special topic is given a key to the school building and to the library or laboratory or studio where he is working. For another, the library is not built around the old system of study tables, but consists of carrels for individual work. If the ardor produced is "just Hawthorne effect," and I doubt it, then maybe nongraded schools should go all out for a permanent Hawthorne effect. It may be that they are doing just this, for the system seems to require chronic innovation by its very nature. Team teaching, for example, is a necessity. Phase organization of courses requires that teachers take a hand in a course, depending on what they do best. And as students move, prepare special papers, or pursue independent studies, they are encouraged to see the teacher who knows the topic best.

Such "reforms" have a way of sounding too administrative.

There is obviously something far deeper than administrative skill or decisiveness in the multiphased arrangement. At the heart of the matter is a sense of intellectual style, a confidence in the ability of students to learn, and a respect for the disorderly ways in which people come by their insights. Dr. Brown describes the curriculum as "concept centered." "The primary purpose of education is the development of the intellect. All other aims and objectives are subordinate." The courses are hard and challenging, and achievement is emphasized. Finally, would one get support for such a program in every community? Probably not, but many communities are ready to take the leap.

I find one special lesson in Frank Brown's book. Many of the best curriculum projects have rested their case on the importance of inquiry, structure, discovery, and independent thinking. Drop a bright new curriculum into a dull school atmosphere, and its glint can be quickly tarnished. The nongraded school is one that has changed the atmosphere of learning to conform to the spirit of the new curricula—from keys to the library to report cards that are your own to dispose of. Inventions have a way of cultivating support. The multiphased ungraded school is one that supports the inventive new work on curricula going on around the country. Like all social inventions, it has a power to liberate human energy to an astonishing degree—and it is this that makes it so promising.

One final personal note. It is so plain, visiting the classrooms of the Melbourne High School, that students are taking major responsibility for their own education. It is this autonomous spirit that most characteristically reflects the student's reaction to the responsibility the school has given him to move at his own pace. There is a pride in the atmosphere. The would-be mechanic, clever with motors but slow with letters, saying "If I'm going to find how these new motors work, I'm going to have to read the manual." Or the girl, headed for practical nursing, wanting to get her writing, "to where you can keep your record sheets right." Or the seminar in American History debating what is an historical fact and considering that it mattered little if you could use them somehow. There is an alertness, an activity about the enterprise that is admirable.

JEROME S. BRUNER
President
American Psychological Association

CONTENTS

THE DISADVANTAGED STUDENT AND THE
NONGRADED PROCESS (CONT.)

propriate curriculum for uncommitted learners.
Varying the curriculum. Linking the curriculum to
the individual. The new physical environment. The
concept of the carrel. The reading laboratory. The
mathematics laboratory. The history laboratory.
Science for uncommitted learners. Time, space, and
matter. Curriculum strategy. Emerging techniques
for involving uncommitted learners. Pointers for effective small group discussions. The importance of
placement. Conclusion.

THE
APPROPRIATE
PLACEMENT
SCHOOL:
A Sophisticated Nongraded Curriculum

Chapter One

THE SCHOOL DESIGNED
FOR FLEXIBLE LEARNING

A REVOLUTION IN ORGANIZATION

Harold Taylor, Vice President of the National Committee for
the Support of Public Schools, recently asserted, "it is the
public elementary and secondary schools that most urgently
are in need of repair." Taylor expects the repair bill will be
high; however, he maintains that the money "is there—it is
simply being spent on other things, from cosmetics and ciga-
rettes to funerals and missiles." [1]

---

[1] *Newsweek*, December 23, 1963, p. 71.

We concur with Mr. Taylor that the public schools are in a serious state of intellectual disrepair, but we heartily disagree that the solution to the problem is no more than an increase in the budget. This book is based on the premise that what the schools need most is not simply more money, but radical and revolutionary internal changes.

Scholars estimate that the rate at which man acquires knowledge doubled for the first time at about 1700, again around 1900; the third doubling occurred about 1950, and the fourth in 1960. If it is true that we are now gathering new knowledge at such an astounding pace that we are doubling the world's gross supply of information every ten years, then the educational process may soon find itself under overwhelming stress. New ways of learning must be rapidly developed and installed in the schools if we are to maintain an intellectual balance between the acquisition and the absorption of new knowledge. It is in this setting that the idea of a nongraded Appropriate Placement school has begun to take shape.

What is an Appropriate Placement school? Why do we need it? The answers to these questions are best seen when focused against the alterations wrought on the structure of society by modern technology.

In the 1800's, when educators first set up the pattern for America's public schools, the frame of reference was a fixed and unyielding society. It was in this severely uncompromising setting that the founders of the nation's schools chose the age of the child as the common denominator for class organization.

The stationary nature of the society of these early educational planners was the underlying factor which caused them to provide a Procrustean system of education composed of rigid component parts. Procrustes, it will be remembered, was the legendary Greek robber who tortured his victims by placing them on a bed; if they were too short, he stretched them to fit;

if they were too long, he cut them down to the proper size. In a fashion similar to the ancient robber's, the intent of the early schools was to assure that learning would be uniform for all students. These pioneer schools were called "graded" schools and the idea of "graded" education soon became an American institution.

The Influence of Technology

The technology of the 1960's has created a society which is far from stable. Spectacular breakthroughs in science and computer technology have generated an atmosphere of rapid and accelerating change. Evidence of a changing society may be seen at every turn. The urbanization process is going on the world over. This is in effect the modernization process. The metropolis has become the vast urban megalopolis. The university responsible to one community has become a multiversity serving many communities. Even the relatively new concept of automation is giving way to a newer process called cybernation. Servo-mechanics is not far away.

In this highly fluid frame of reference, the image of "graded" education has become debilitated. Curriculum planners are frantically seeking to design a more flexible system. The endeavors to modernize and innovate have made age as the criterion for grouping hopelessly obsolete.

The new class organization which offers the most accommodation to individual learning is the innovation utilizing the *achievement* of students—not age—as the index for setting up classes. Achievement supplants age as the criterion for advancement. For want of a better name, this remodeled arrangement of grouping students was originally called the "nongraded" plan.

This new *modus operandi* can no longer be properly called a nongraded school. The nongraded school implies a change in school organization with minor curriculum adjustments. In its more sophisticated form, the nongraded school has become the Appropriate Placement school. This is a revolutionary new organization which calls for both a new organization and a corresponding revolution in curriculum.

The Bankruptcy of Graded Education

In the contemporary industrial and social setting, the schools can no longer afford to be indifferent to change. The motionless state of the curriculum of the conventionally graded school can be compared to the Irish woman in 1939 who had just heard of the first World War. Bristling with indignation, the lady said: "And wasn't it terrible for the King of Germany to declare war on the King of England, and him so unprepared and all!"

In the same vein, advocates of graded education are denouncing the introduction of new innovations, saying in effect, "and us so unprepared and all." Supporters of change by cautious evolution would have us look upon the *status quo* in education as if it were high wisdom in a white suit. To resist change, conventional school administrators are coming out with a re-hash of the traditional curricula. This can only be described as a counter revolution.

Most of the material being taught in graded schools is already lifeless. For example, the graded curriculum ignores the great themes of subjects. Graded curricula are composed largely of particulars and in graded classes students are largely engulfed with details. Tiny bits of information, unrelated to major concepts, fail to give students the incentive needed for curiosity and inquiry. By perpetuating this attitude, graded education has lost most of its vitality.

What is needed is an educational earthquake, and the first upheaval should break into pieces the outdated method of grouping youngsters into grades on the basis of chronological age. The graded school was developed in 1537 as a solution to the grouping problems of the 16th century. It has cursed education ever since.

The History of Graded Education

A brief glance at the history of the graded school is basic to an understanding of the serious debacle of school organization. The idea of the graded school is medieval. It was first conceived by a Prussian schoolmaster named John Sturum while he was teaching in a Gymnasium at Strassburg. Sturum's school has been described as follows:

> The pupils were expected to spend a year in each one of the nine classes, each class having its own teacher, its regular course of study, and its examination for promotion, about as in the graded schools of today which have not broken away from these medieval methods. Sturum not only apportioned a certain amount to be accomplished in a given time, as nearly all do now, but he even forbade them to learn anything else. These ideas of his were transmitted from the sixteenth century to the nineteenth century by means of the Jesuit schools and the secondary schools of Continental Europe.[2]

The distinguished Massachusetts Commissioner of Education, Horace Mann, visited Europe in the 1840's and was much impressed with the Prussian graded schools. It was through his persuasion that the new Quincy grammer school in Boston opened its doors in 1848 as the first graded school in America. Principal Philbrick wrote about the Quincy school:

> The essential features consisted first in giving a separate room to each teacher; second, in grouping a sufficient number of these rooms in the same building to accommodate pupils enough for a good classification.[3]

---

[2] William J. Shearer, *The Grading of Schools,* New York: H. P. Smith Publishing Company, 1899, p. 20.

[3] John D. Philbrick, *City School System in the United States.* Washington, D. C., U. S. Government Printing Office, 1885, p. 158.

Elwood P. Cubberly, the great historian of Education at Stanford University, described the impact of the Quincy grammer school: "More than any other single influence it stimulated the introduction of the graded classroom form of school organization." [4]

Near the latter part of the nineteenth century, considerable opposition built up to the rigidity and pervasiveness of the graded schools. The first great champion of what he called "ungraded" schools was William J. Shearer, Superintendent of Schools of the City of Elizabeth, N. J. Shearer reported in 1898 that many schools had tried to inaugurate an ungraded system but were not ingenious enough to plan this kind of a program because of the increasingly large numbers of students entering school. In a prophetic book, *The Grading of Schools,* Shearer wrote that a more rational plan of grouping students than that used in the graded school was the most pressing issue of the times.

The idea of an ungraded school goes back to the turn of the century, but Shearer's ideas were not translated into action until the mid-1930's when a few school systems began to experiment with the ungraded primary plan.

And now, let me spell out what is wrong with the graded school. The graded school is frozen to a dangerously dated posture. Its monolithic structure is rigged against sound learning. The curriculum is designed to meet group demands, and it does this with Procrustean solutions. As often as not the effect of the graded school is to bring uncommitted learners into contact with an incompatible curriculum. Graded schools are still flunking 25% of the students and blaming the students for their failure. In nearly every way, the graded school has been extremely moderate when it should be moderately extreme. Whitehead once remarked that a merely well-informed

---

[4] Elwood P. Cubberly, *Public Education in the United States.* New York: Houghton Mifflin Company, 1934, p. 311.

man is the worst bore on earth, yet in the curriculum of the graded schools we treat youngsters as if they were an input and retrieval system. The graded school curriculum is, at best, a disorderly network of learning. It is a bureaucracy designed for children.

Conventional school administrators treat the embalmed credo of the graded school as if it were the only way to approach learning. Furthermore, textbook authors and publishers have put millions of new little pieces into graded curricula, but have done little actually to justify the system. It is not, however, necessary to recite the entire litany here. Suffice it to say that it is time we stopped chain smoking ourselves to death with chronological age grouping. If we continue the present trend of evolving curriculum materials to fit the obsolete graded school organization, then we shall be retreading very thin rubber. A vulcanized, patched curriculum is hardly appropriate to the age of cyberculture.

The Variegation of Subject Matter

When the educational process is loosened, learning is approached in violently different ways. Subject matter for some consists of studying the basic skills. For others, subject matter is almost entirely problem solving. The object of Appropriate Placement is to provide a curriculum with differing variations. The intent of the curriculum in this school is to jar students by the unexpected: to force them to an unusual or creative response by a condition of uncertainty. The purpose is to activate curiosity, which is excited when a reasonable amount of uncertainty is introduced into a learning situation. If too little uncertainty is initiated, students may become bored; when too much is brought in they become frustrated. The skillful teacher knows just how much uncertainty to bring into the learning situation.

The progress of education can only be in the direction of

the Appropriate Placement School, for there is simply no other direction to take. The entire purpose of Appropriate Placement is to educate for flexibility. The placement process is designed to give students flexibility of attitude and mind. In an era of unparalleled breakthroughs in science and computer technology, individuals must have a "built in" kind of expertise with which they can quickly acquire new skills when old skills are automated away. Present trends indicate that the average individual will need to be re-trained three times as a result of the inroads of automation. This calls for a ground swell in the direction of flexible education.

During its gradual evolution, the American educational system has not been geared for working with students who have a high creative potential. As simple evidence: where in this country can one find a school, public or private, which has a place on its report cards for marking students on the basis of creative achievement? Certainly not in New York or California, states which pride themselves on their good schools. In education by evolution, much has been written and said about scholastic excellence. In revolutionized education much is being written about curiosity and imagination, as types of excellence, but unfortunately these are types which graded schools have indeed neglected. Schools have always recognized, nourished, and applauded academic excellence, but there has been no reward or recognition for curiosity, an ability which might lead students to learn what they are not expected to know. Faced with the enormous problem of educating boys and girls for professions which do not yet exist and cannot now be described, education must be revolutionized at least to the point of producing individuals who are adaptable to change. If we fail to educate individuals to live in a rapidly changing society then they will not be able to deal effectively with the flexible future.

The new technology kindled by Sputnik has spilled over

into all aspects of our daily lives, and the spirit of change is pervasive everywhere. This means that it is no longer possible for the schools to stand on one foot while evolving new ideas one step at a time. The educational enterprise is fast re-tooling and gearing to educate the most creative generation which the world has yet produced. New approaches in education will seem fantastic, even mad to those who view educational change in a traditional perspective. Once we acquire the courage, the imagination, and the motivation to use the knowledge and technology which is at our disposal, we can revolutionize our educational system in such fashion that we will be achieving the same procession of breakthroughs in education as we find in our science and technology.

General Principles of Flexibility

If the schools are ever to meet the needs of students, then the curriculum must be tailored to the huge range of abilities which youth represents. In an appropriate curriculum, all boys and girls should have the opportunity to study subjects and processes in which they can be successful. Quality education can be said to exist only when the best possible education is available at the varying levels at which the students in the school are able to perform. The entire curriculum should not be within the range of all students, but some part of the curriculum should be within the realm of the possible for each student. These aims are not to be achieved in the stratified organization of the grade.

And so we must look ahead at another rationale. In the Appropriate Placement arrangement, the most important part of the process is the achievement and potential of each individual. The object is to provide a curriculum exquisitely tailored to the requirements of the individual student. Unless the curriculum is specifically constructed on the basis of the needs of students, it is not appropriate; and, in the past, too much of the curriculum has been just that. A competent system of education may be said to exist only when all students are in programs consistent with, and challenging to, their abilities. As I pointed out earlier, the major block to improving public education is not financial support, as entrenched interests advocate. The major obstacle is the rigid organization that has been even further regimented by scheduling students into a certain number of periods within a particular grade rather than into a desirable program of studies. Conventional school scheduling seems to have been designed largely for the purpose of getting students out of the hall at certain times. The result is a "misfit" brand of education, which is being administered to large numbers of students. The idea of placement in a curriculum appropriate to the individual, however, is much more than just a change in the organizational process. It advocates a shift in the intent of the educational program. The changed direction comprises a giant step from rigidity toward extreme flexibility. The Appropriate Placement school champions a move from a curriculum for the group to a curriculum for the individual. At the far end of the swing of the nongraded pendulum is the exotic concept of learning so highly individualized that some students will receive their education by appointment.

The Difficult Forty Percent

While the process of Appropriate Placement sharpens and improves the organization of learning for all students, the gains are simply enormous in the education of those students whose achievement lies in the lower forty percent of the school population. In the graded school, this group has become known as the "difficult forty percent" because they have long since lost interest in school. Their education has consisted largely of their physical presence in the classroom. Part of the cause of this vast loss of interest is the fact that the public system of education has consistently put its major emphasis on college preparatory programs, while the greater number of students has not gone to college. The chief concern of the educational establishment must be to develop in each individual his highest potential.

The Chemistry of Learning

Past attempts to discover the process by which children learn have put all of their emphasis upon the psychology of learning. But now, after a hundred years of educational psychology, we still do not have an adequate idea how children learn. For example, we do not know why spelling is easy for one child and difficult for another coming from the same background, even the same family. Although some gains have been made, the absence of practical results in the psychology of learning point dramatically to the failure of educational psychology: after a century, no competent body of knowledge exists in this field. The really significant contribution of educational psychology to learning is in the field of testing, but much of this is now in disrepute. Psychology's greatest discovery, the I.Q., is no longer considered to be of much significance, yet educational psychologists have failed to develop anything new. Both secondary schools and colleges are desperately in need of a new kind of standard which will enable them better to select and group students for learning. In view of this, Dean Eugene S. Wilson of Amherst College conceives of a Q.Q. (Quest Quotient) structured to estimate the individual's ability to learn new skills when old skills are cybernated away. Either a Q.Q. or an S.Q. (Skills Quotient) would be superior to the imponderable I.Q.

The plight of educational psychology is such that educational psychologists are no longer able to tailor education to fit their theories. The result is that the field of educational psychology is in a state of intellectual impotence. Instead of being artful and advancing new ideas, the educationalists are standing like a sleeping stork on one foot. An educational psychologist, defending the controversial concentration of experimentation in psychology on rats and mice as the key to learning, was recently overheard to admit, "Rats are on their way out." Where learning is concerned, I would like to predict that educational psychology is on its way out. It is time to replace the confusing theories of educational psychology with a major effort to develop a chemistry of learning. We are much closer to breakthroughs in biochemical knowledge about human learning than we are to discoveries in educational psychology. Through bio-chemistry, perhaps we can take up where the educationalist has failed, and at last discover what is physically involved in the learning process. Definitive experiments in the chemistry of learning have determined that the abilities of even the slowest student in the school are vastly greater than most people assume. They have further ascertained that even young students are capable of much deeper involvement in learning than was previously thought. This exciting discovery calls for penetrating new ventures in learning. These can be only in the direction of the Appropriate Placement plan which calls for conventional curricula to be drastically overhauled to present a new rationale of education.

The Appropriate Placement Program

Many educators are under the false impression that an Appropriate Placement school is no more than a different way of grouping students. They could hardly be more wrong. The school system which is interested only in grouping students differently should not undertake new models of placement. The purpose of the Appropriate Placement Program is (1) to schedule learning at the student's past accomplishment level and (2) to feed ideas and learning at the individual student's level of understanding. Once the school commits itself to the notion of Appropriate Placement it must immediately undertake several major renovations in its method of operation.

(1) It must rid itself of textbooks written for a particular grade level. These materials are not adaptable to the new grouping by achievement and no attempt should be made to make them so. They simply will not do.

(2) New materials must be devised which link subject matter to the particular achievement level of each student.

(3) The teaching staff must re-examine its function in order to teach more effectively.

Each of these items will be examined separately, since they are all important components of the new process of individual student placement.

Subject Matter Content

Since textbooks currently in use have been written to be used at a particular grade level, they are not suitable for a curriculum which is geared for individual learning. The anatomy of the Appropriate Placement school requires material more carefully fashioned to the achievement level of the individual. For students who have failed to learn basic skills, nongraded material must deal with essential principles. Past efforts to educate youngsters with learning gaps have centered around using materials from lower grades. Lower grade material is not relevant for older students who have become disadvantaged by their failure to learn. Students encumbered by a learning handicap need new material constructed on elementary principles, but with components of sophisticated interest. For the curriculum of more able students, an important source of new material is found in the vast array of paperback books which is flooding the market. Many nongraded schools offer paperbacks for sale in the school library, while others have set up paperback book stores within the school. Paperback materials, in addition to being inexpensive, have several distinct advantages over standard textbooks. When textbooks are furnished by the school system, the student can neither underline nor make marks in them. In other words, he cannot really *use* them. It is, of course, important for a student to be able to underscore thoughts which interest him and to write his own ideas in the margin of the book. In addition, whenever a student buys a book, he is beginning to acquire his own library, which puts him in the habit of possessing books.

Educational Services Incorporated

The most useful curriculum materials that are being developed today are those originating from the laboratories of Educational Services Incorporated, a subsidiary of the Massachusetts Institute of Technology. E.S.I.'s most important production so far is the new physics course commonly called the P.S.S.C. physics. The organization is currently in the process of inventing new materials for high school social studies, elementary science, and elementary mathematics. All of the materials of Education Services Incorporated utilize the *discovery approach* advocated by Jerome S. Bruner.[5]

The Teacher Must Change

The Appropriate Placement of students calls for extreme changes in the manner in which teachers are assigned to work with students. In the past, talented teachers have been assigned exclusively to gifted students. If we are ever going to solve the irritating problems of the drop-out, the deprived, or the segregated, then we must bring some of the talented forces in the school to bear upon the learning problems of the disadvantaged learner. Students who have deep-seated learning problems cannot learn from inexperienced and below average

---

[5] Jerome S. Bruner, *The Process of Education,* Boston: Harvard University Press, 1963.

teachers. These youngsters must be taught in smaller classes and by extremely able teachers. In effect, whenever a student falls behind in one of the *basic* subjects, his class size must be cut and he must be assured of an able and talented teacher. It is a major problem to interest extremely able teachers in extremely unable students. What is needed are some administrators who will play Robin Hood by taking some of the teachers from the rich and talented and giving them to the poor and untalented.

As his role changes, the teacher will lecture only when he has something important and specific to say; otherwise, his function will be to lead discussions, encourage research, assist with individual projects, and help counsel students having special problems.

The Structure of Subjects

Conceptual logistics gives the curriculum of the nongraded school a vastly different structure from that of the graded school. Graded school curricula are based on the idea of chronological learning. In the nongraded school, the concept of chronological learning is rejected. Instead, students are led to discover the major themes which hold the subject together. The curriculum emphasis in the Appropriate Placement school is on the structure of the discipline. By this I mean that the student should begin the study of a subject with an attitude of inquiry. His approach should be in the same inquiring fashion as the original developers of the subject.

The two main objectives in studying a subject are: (1) the immediate pleasure derived from the effort; and (2) the importance of this effort to the student in the future. At first glance these goals may seem loosely conceived, but there has been entirely too much absolutism in school curricula. The objectives of pleasure and profit as criteria for studying a subject get right at the heart of what learning should be. America's leading learning theorist, Professor Bruner, has concentrated on the structure and logistics of curricula. He writes about basic structure:

> Designing curricula in a way that reflects the basic structure of a field of knowledge requires the most fundamental understanding of that field. It is a task that cannot be carried out without the active participation of the ablest scholars and scientists. The experience of the past several years has shown that such scholars and scientists, working in conjunction with experienced teachers and students of child development, can prepare curricula of the sort we have been considering. Much more effort in the actual preparation of curriculum materials, in teacher training, and in supporting research will be necessary if improvements in our educational practices are to be of an order that will meet the challenges of the scientific and social revolution through which we are now living.[6]

The nature of a subject has considerable bearing upon how it is treated in the curriculum of the school. For example, science has been far more successful than other subjects in springing students from the classroom into the freedom of self-propelled intellectual activity. There are several reasons why more high school students are pursuing science under conditions of freedom and independence than any other subject. First of all, great themes which hold the subject together are more easily identified. Also, laboratory work requires independent observation and experimentation. But most important, science lends itself more easily to the exciting *discovery approach* to problem solving. The importance of students' learning through the process of discovery is well treated in the carefully written but not very subtle reply of a renowned scientist to the request for information from the daughter of an

---

[6] *Ibid.*, p. 32.

old friend. The Professor's reply, which has been widely printed in professional journals as "Letter to Virginia," is of particular interest here.

LETTER TO VIRGINIA

Dear Virginia:

You ask me for "any information you might have on bacteria harmful to man." Since I have spent my life on this subject, and so did my father before me, and since I am, I am sure, older than your father and mother, I cannot send you all the information I have without sending you my library and writing a book for you.

The best I can do is to send you a book under separate cover, which you can put in your library when you are through with it, either your own or in school. I am also sending an article I wrote about this kind of question, which I hope you will give to your teacher. Possibly he or she will not like it, so tell him or her that you are not to blame.

Teachers are trying to stir up in you an interest in what goes on about you, but teachers have fallen in bad ways in some of the things they do. If they told you how to use the library or helped you find a book and to read it, then you would be growing with your learning. Even when they teach you to write a pleasant and correct letter, perhaps you learn something, though I think you can figure this out for yourself.

But, when they get you to ask someone to do your work for you, then they are robbing you of a chance to do your own discovering by thinking, by searching, and by studying. They are teaching you to depend on others when you are just learning to enjoy depending on yourself. If this goes on, you will become not only dependent on someone else all the time, which is no fun and is not necessary, but also you will find yourself believing everything you are told, without thinking, and what you are told will not always be as good as something you thought out for yourself. You do not want to be a checker, being pushed around all your life over a checkerboard. You want to be the one who plays checkers, and wins some of the time.

I am trying to help you with your project, but help a

little more than that. My students are mostly 24 years old or about that, and I get not only letters like yours, but I see what happens when students subjected to this sort of thing try to do advanced work. Some of them still think that, if they telephone to someone and ask a question, they have performed a great mental task. You be the one to whom they telephone, not the one who does the telephoning.

Sincerely,
Max S. Marshall, Chairman
Department of Microbiology [7]

Learning Must Be Heuristic

Another dimension to the escalator-like curriculum of the nongraded school is the need for greater profundity in the classroom. Teachers must strive to evoke heuristic responses from students. The word heuristic is derived from the Greek word *heuriskin*, meaning "to find and observe." A heuristic response is one in which the student will continue to investigate and find out for himself. Sample questions of this technique are:

What would the world be like if light traveled the way smoke does?

Why were the early settlers able to enslave the African Negro, but unable to enslave the woodland Indian?

When students acquire highly developed heuristic skills, we will find that a higher proportion of knowledge will be gained from a given amount of factual information.

Education Has Been Too Passive

While it may appear that this chapter has theorized rather brazenly about a burgeoning new concept in education, this is not the case at all when one considers the wave of dissatisfaction which is facing the conventionally graded school. With

---

[7] Dr. Max S. Marshall, University of California Medical Center, San Francisco, California. *Peabody Educational Journal,* May 1961.

increasing animosity, parents are raising the question: "Why is there a block to learning in the school situation for a child who learns very readily outside the school?" Actually, learning is something that youngsters do naturally. *It takes tremendous ingenuity to keep them from it.* The solution to the problem is simple. The impulse of the school system has been to make individuals passive. Education has been too restrictive, limiting intellectual development to the requirements of the grade level. The process of graded education is stratified—it attempts to educate youngsters in layers. The organization of the school should long ago have been reshaped to allow students to be selective on the basis of their past accomplishments.

Up to now the schools have been unwilling to change their curricula except when supported by the largesse of foundations. The result is that the curriculum of the traditional graded school has walled itself into a *cul de sac* from which it is going to be extremely difficult to emerge. In method of grouping, graded schools are immeasurably farther ahead in band and athletics than they are in the academic areas. The consequence is that the graded school is on the verge of becoming a disaster area. Graded education is an educational calamity which is leading us toward intellectual bankruptcy.

The Ungraded College

The big problem is that the school organization has never been properly engineered. The nongraded school which developed out of opposition to the grade is fast evolving into a new system of flexible placement in which students are scheduled into more appropriate learning situations. Actually, the best colleges in the country are nothing more than ungraded schools. Last fall Amherst College granted advanced placement in foreign languages to almost half of its entering freshmen; of the 300 members of the class 88 were given advanced placement in mathematics and 57 in physics and chemistry. Over a hundred students enter Harvard each year as sophomores as a result of having taken college level work in the secondary school and having earned satisfactory marks on the advanced placement examinations of the College Board.

Mr. Edward T. Wilcox, Director of the Harvard College Program of Advanced Standing, epitomized the nongraded viewpoint at Harvard recently with this statement: "On the whole our admissions committee is now deeply committed to a policy of high diversity in the incoming student body." [8]

The following chart contains statistics which illustrate the extent to which Harvard has become involved in the process of moving students ahead on the basis of their achievement rather than on the old-fashioned notion of numbers of courses and credits.

The Appropriate Placement Plan

The new nongraded model then is patterned after the Advanced Placement Program of the College Entrance Examination Board which gives advanced standing and placement to the more able college freshman. When applied to the high school curriculum, advanced placement becomes Appropriate Placement. In effect, the new organization of the school which began as a nongraded school has moved into the more sophisticated stage of flexible and Appropriate Placement. Appropriate Placement is a serious effort to do something about the evasive problem of individual differences. In brief the principles of the Appropriate Placement Plan are:

(1) All students are placed in courses on the basis of achievement in a particular subject.

(2) Convenient arrangements for mobile learning are built into the curriculum.

---

[8] Letter to author dated March 8, 1965.

ADVANCED PLACEMENT AT HARVARD COLLEGE [9]
1955–1964

Year Entered	Total No. Schools	Total No. Candidates	Candidates Receiving AP	Total* Exams Presented	Total No. Awards	Eligible for Soph Std.	Accepted Soph Std.
1955	39	146	81	193	98	2	2
1956	49	181	122	370	177	13	13
1957	80	264	179	529	295	33	33
1958	116	366	273	738	454	55	55
1959	152	455	386	1119	716	97	84
1960	184	530	398	1349	738	96	88
1961	215	540	452	1388	858	134	103
1962	299	552	480	1361	932	133	101
1963	240	640	520	1669	1090	165	126
1964	282	615	526	1636	1136	190	112

[9] *Advanced Placement* is a nongraded process by which the nation's leading colleges and universities place students on the basis of achievement.

* Examinations in English Comp., Latin 4, and German 4 are not included since they do not lead to Advanced Placement at Harvard. These exams total as follows: '55(64), '56(84), '57(127), '58(194), '59(285), '60(344), '61(27), '62(43), '63(36), '64(27).

Graded Schools Versus Appropriate Placement

At this point it is well to make a sharp comparison between the basic assumptions of the graded school and those of the Appropriate Placement Plan. The graded schools are based upon the following principles: (1) The curriculum prescribes a specific area of subject matter which must be covered. (2) The subject matter in the curriculum is carefully identified and prescribed. (3) Every effort is made to keep learning as sequential as possible. (4) The one role of individual differences is that they influence one's chances in the race to cover the prescribed curriculum.

By contrast the Appropriate Placement School provides for individual differences by (1) grouping students on the basis of achievement; (2) allowing students to progress through the curriculum at their own rate and capacity; (3) allowing individual progress to the point of eliminating grades and sometimes abolishing and instituting new courses; (4) providing individualized scheduling so that the student has considerable freedom in selecting courses tailored to his own interests and rate of learning; (5) considering learning less sequential than previously thought.

"The vertical organization of the school should
provide for the continuous, unbroken, upward progression
of all learners, with due recognition of the wide
variability among learners in every aspect of their
development. The school organization should, therefore,
provide for differentiated rates and means of progression
toward achievement of educational goals.
Nongrading and multigrading are promising
alternatives to the traditional graded school and should
be given careful consideration in seeking to provide
flexible progress plans geared to human variability." [1]

Chapter Two

THE PROCESS OF

MULTIPHASED EDUCATION

Curricular remodeling is not an arduous task, nor is it necessarily a long-range accomplishment. It can take place within a
relatively brief interval of time, provided the people in the
school know what to do.

In spite of the myriad "How-to-do-it" books which have
been published on the subject of curriculum development, we
still do not have a first-class design that teachers and admin-

---

[1] RECOMMENDATION #23. *Schools for the 60's.* A Report of the Project
on Instruction. National Education Association. McGraw-Hill Book Co., Inc.,
1963, p. 132.

istrators can follow in their efforts to revamp the school program. The main problem is that most of the books which deal with the curriculum have been written by professors of education, and too much of their writing is theoretical. Not nearly enough has been written about curriculum technology in the language of direct experience and "nuts and bolts." It is the intent of this chapter to illustrate that reorganizing the rigid graded school into a flexible multiphased Appropriate Placement school is not a complex operation. Indeed, the organization of an Appropriate Placement program provides an efficient and orderly format for making the conversion.

First Steps to Nongrading

The organizational move from graded to nongraded education is anything but intricate. It involves only three simple changes:

1. An expansion of the scope of the present conventionally graded organization so that a "grade" becomes a three-year rather than a one-year concept.
2. A plan for grouping students by achievement rather than age.
3. Discontinuance of the ambiguous term "grade."

The essence of the issue is that the traditional division of the school into twelve grades should be converted into four zones of learning. Each zone should encompass the equivalent of three grades. The new three-year spans of learning which are formed should have the specific objective of providing a new structure for a more highly individualized curriculum. They are, in effect, nongraded areas based on multiphased curricula.

The re-designed organization of the school into four multiphased zones of learning is as follows:

The Multiphased Primary School
The Multiphased Intermediate School
The Multiphased Junior High School
The Multiphased Senior High School

The curricula within each multiphased zone should be re-built around the achievement of students rather than the grade to which they have been promoted. Subject matter geared to achievement is far more appropriate and flexible than that centered around the grade level.

The New Shape of the Curriculum

The purpose of multiphasing the school is to allow the introduction of a new curriculum carefully coupled to the learning needs of the individual. The Appropriate Placement Plan is based on the premise that the curriculum of each individual must be determined by his already acquired understanding of a particular discipline. This differs radically from the philosophy of the graded school, which is based entirely on a student's past experiences in a discipline rather than his established knowledge of the subject.

In the curriculum of the school built around four zones of learning, each student's ability to comprehend and grasp a particular stage of learning must be ascertained before he is assigned to a class. The system requires that every student be tested on the basis of achievement in the basic areas of language arts, mathematics, science, and history. Nationally standardized tests are used. The cresting point of the student's previous achievement in each subject must be definitely established in order that he can be precisely scheduled into specific learning situations to meet his individual requirements.

It is important to emphasize that achievement tests must be the major instrument used in re-deploying students out of the grade and into an appropriate multiphased zone. The I.Q. is not a reliable enough predictive factor to be of any value; achievement tests, on the other hand, are reasonably effective. Actually, the I.Q. is so unreliable that group I.Q. tests were recently abolished in New York City. In making this announcement, Deputy Superintendent Joseph Loretan told New York City principals that group I.Q. tests "can present a misleading picture of a student's abilities resulting in an inappropriate instructional program." New York has replaced I.Q. tests with achievement tests.

Phased Learning

The system of bonding the curriculum to the needs of the individual is called *phased learning*. A phase is a flexible learning situation which is related directly to the achievement of the student rather than to the grade to which he has been promoted. Expressed in another way, a phase is a stage of development with a varying time element. A student who learns in a modest fashion will remain in a phase indefinitely, even a year or more. On the other hand, a rapid learner will move through several phases within a relatively short span of time. The whole notion of phasing is dedicated to the idea of change and constant advance. The purpose is to provide a more flexible learning situation better designed to accommodate individual learning.

In the multiphased curriculum all students are scheduled by depth of learning rather than by the system of chronological age and annual promotion, which is used in the graded school. A description of class situations created by the new multiphased structure of learning is as follows:

THE MULTIPHASED CURRICULUM

Phase 1—Subjects are provided for students who perform from 0 to 20th percentile on standardized achievement tests, indicating that they need special assistance in small classes.

Phase 2—Subjects are organized for students who range between the 20th and 40th percentile in achievement and who need more emphasis on fundamentals.

Phase 3—Courses are arranged for students who score between the 40th and 60th percentile on standardized achievement tests, indicating that they have an average background of accomplishment.

Phase 4—Subject matter is planned for extremely well prepared students who achieve between the 60th and
80th percentiles and desire education in depth.

Phase 5—Courses are available for students who attain above
the 80th percentile and are willing to assume responsibility for their own learning, pursuing college level
courses while still in high school.

Phase Q—Students whose creative talents are well developed
should give consideration to the Quest phase of the
curriculum. This is an important dimension of the
phased organization which gives thrust in the direction of individual fulfillment. In this phase, a student
may research any area in which he is deeply and
sincerely interested.

In a flexible multiphased curriculum, student learning is deliberately varied and highly individualized. For example, one
student may be programmed into Phase 1 for social studies
(achievement below the 20th percentile), Phase 2 for language
arts (achievement between the 20th and 40th percentiles),
Phase 3 for science (achievement between the 40th and 60th
percentiles), and Phase 4 for mathematics (achievement between the 60th and 80th percentiles).

Since reading is the most important subject in the curriculum
and mathematics is second, a student's needs in these areas
must receive special attention. Whenever a student falls behind in reading or mathematics, he must be scheduled for extra
time in this subject. Furthermore, this increased time must
be provided in a small class where students can receive as
much personal attention as is needed to learn the subject
thoroughly.

The Appropriate Placement Plan of organization offers a
major step in a new direction for the educational enterprise.
But this is not enough. The role of the teacher must change to
meet the dynamics of a changed establishment. The teacher
must radically revise her techniques in this new approach to

more individualized learning. I am talking here about the monotonous practice in which the teacher conducts a class by asking questions to which she has standard answers. This technique has become so thoroughly ingrained as a method of pedagogy that the publishers of some school materials prepare canned questions supplied to teachers in manuals accompanying the textbook. This kind of teaching is too ineffective to be useful in the classroom of a multiphased school.

The Mission of Teaching in the Multiphased Curriculum

While it is extremely important to allow the individual teacher flexibility of method in obtaining the goals of the course, there are several basic principles to which she must adhere in the multiphased program:

1. Presentation of materials comprises approximately 20% of the time in the course. (This includes time spent in viewing films as well as lecturing.)
2. Discussion in analysis groups constitutes approximately 40% of the class time.
3. Individual work and reading encompasses roughly 40% of the class time.

Each of these functions is discussed separately in order to illustrate how they are accomplished.

Presentation of Materials (Twenty percent of class time)

One of the major stumbling blocks to learning in the junior and senior high school is over-using the lecture as a method of teaching. In its earliest beginnings the profession of teaching began with the lecture method, since before the textbook and the seminar this way was the only way to communicate knowledge. The effectiveness of the lecture technique has declined as new and more sophisticated methods of teaching have been developed. Compulsory education laws have also contributed enormously to outmoding the lecture. The intellectually elite can profit from lecture teaching, but the general population does not learn well this way. As the cultural interests of the nation increased, school laws brought into the schools the general population with their comparatively lower range of abilities. For them, lectures are unprofitable unless they are kept quite short. As a matter of fact, this method of teaching would have disappeared a decade ago had it not been for the new emphasis given it by the team teaching movement.

The lecture, as a manner of presentation, is far more appropriate to the setting of the college where the learning structure is radically different from that of the high school. College students usually have no more than two or three classes a day; high school students must face from five to eight. There is a decided limit to the amount of learning which can be absorbed through the process of being "talked to," and furthermore most high school teachers do not have the background and training to sustain a truly interesting lecture, while a college teacher usually does. The lecture, as an effective learning experience for college students, is further strengthened by a subtle type of motivation which arises from an awareness that their parents are paying a high price for their education. And, of course, college students are a highly select group. The essence of the matter is that the student body of colleges differs vastly, both in intellect and sophistication, from the general population which comes within the province of the high school. No more than one-third of the current school population is college bound, and, in many public schools, another one-third of the students are seriously handicapped by cultural disadvantages. Since high school learning activities must deal with the general population, learning at this level should be organized around a more participatory activity in which the student is personally involved. The rare exceptions are in the few high schools which deal only with pre-college students.

The Role of the Lecture in Team Teaching

The problems with the lecture are largely ignored in the principles of the team teaching movement. The result is that a serious threat to learning arises in modern team teaching situations where a committee of teachers insists upon lecturing 40 percent of the time as prescribed in the original principles of team teaching. Unfortunately, this movement has selected television as its model, with the result that its appeal is as a mass medium. Team teaching is effective only when the lecture (which includes all viewing and listening) is limited to about 10 percent of the time. The majority of class time should be spent in the shirt-sleeve learning of small group discussions and individual study. Personal involvement is the key to learning in the secondary school.

Conclusions About the Lecture

The lecture is the most inferior of the methods of teaching used in the high school. The length of the school day is never less than six hours in length, and in many schools students are "lectured to" for this whole time. This is poor teaching, and the result is poor learning. The lecture is a passive approach to learning, and high school students need active engagement. In the Appropriate Placement Program the maximum time allowed for presentation of materials never exceeds twenty percent of the time set aside for the course. This includes not only the time spent in lecturing but also the time utilized in the viewing of films and closed-circuit television.

Analysis Groups (Forty percent of class time)

In the conventional classroom, the student has been trained to believe that his teacher is right and accepts what she has to say without question. This is not the case when students communicate in shirt-sleeve group discussions with their peers.

A student is much more inclined to think critically about an idea expressed by a fellow student than about something from his teacher. The parry and thrust of discussion among students who are near equals in achievement gives needed practice in critical and analytical thinking. In peer discussion, ideas can be developed on a plane that is close to the student's level of understanding. Students must learn to question, to weigh and analyze evidence freighted with conflicting opinion. The situation which provides the best training in this takes place when students are allowed to tackle problems as peers in analysis groups. Analysis group interaction between students opens up a large pool of ideas to the individual.

The intent of the analysis group technique is to teach through posed problems rather than giving easy solutions. An analysis group consists of from 5 to 8 students who have been given an important problem to discuss and analyze. When I speak of analysis groups, I am not referring to the general discussion group which is used in team teaching. The team teaching group consists of from 12 to 15 students—too many for a profitable discussion. The result is general conversation which is at best only a light-weight intellectual activity. I am talking about a sincere analysis of the problem through definite steps leading to a solution.

The steps for tackling a problem by use of analysis groups are:

1. A succinct statement of the problem.
2. Analysis of the problems through discussion.
3. Assignment of priorities.
4. Formation of preferred and alternative solutions.

Individual Work (Forty percent of class time)

Each individual must spend an increasing amount of time learning for himself. This is the best and most exciting learning of all. Advanced students should spend time working on individual projects in laboratories, in "quest-centers," and in reading sophisticated materials. The more modest learners must engage in vastly different kinds of learning, but their activities can be just as highly individualized. The diffident learner can concentrate on basic skills through individualized reading machines and tape recorders. In schools which show respect for individual competencies and needs, the range of activities for individual learnings is enormous. In this setting the role of the teacher changes from a dispenser of facts to the director of a new and exciting process of learning.

In the conventional classroom, individual imagination has been too severely disciplined. The teaching staff must now set in motion a new kind of teaching—one centered around imagination, intuitive thinking, and inquiry. The major effort must concentrate on developing students who can perceive with discrimination. The success of individual work is contingent upon the selection by the student of a problem worthy of investigation. Albert Einstein once said that the characteristic of a great scientist was his ability to ask nature the right question. The right question for most students is one where the answer can be sought with material and intellectual resources which are available.

Radical Curriculum Revision

The greatest enigma confronting education is the puzzle of how ordinary teachers can teach ordinary students in an extraordinary way. The pieces of the puzzle are beginning to fit into place as youngsters are placed in more flexible and productive learning situations.

It is largely through the efforts of Educational Services Incorporated that curriculum revision is now attracting the interest of professional scholars whose participation is giving the schools a new kind of course structured around the basic principles of the subject. It is expected that in the near future all curricula will be written by scholars, and school systems will give up the practice of having teachers prepare elaborate curriculum guides. It is significant that E. S. I.'s new curricula are based on the premise that the educational process is a continuum and no portion of it may be treated in isolation from the rest. This is a far cry from the philosophy of the past in which textbook writers have traditionally developed separate unrelated units for each grade level.

The New Role of the Teacher

New developments have changed the function of the teacher. Instead of the teacher's controlling the classroom by asking questions to which he has routine answers, his task is to develop profound questions which involve the major themes that hold the subject together. These questions should be carefully designed to encourage students to search on their own. Exciting questions proposed by the teacher are tackled in a balanced program of small group discussions and individual research, making the process of learning the act of discovery.

The Analytic Process

Graded schools emphasize an analytic approach to learning, which proceeds in an orderly fashion one step at a time. Each step is specifically related to the previous step. This kind of teaching is easily handled by the schools since each step is exact and has clear limits. The analytic approach is such a well defined process that practically all graded school curricula are based on it; the very simplicity of its step-by-step approach has caused schools to saddle themselves with sequential, one-step-at-a-time teaching. Current research is beginning to report that most learning is not sequential at all. New materials based on major principles which may not be sequential in either detail or ideas are needed to interest and challenge the student's creative imagination.

Intuitive Thinking

In contrast to the analytical step-by-step approach to knowledge is the intuitive leap by which the solution to a problem is conceived through intelligent guessing. The student literally skips over the data which might lead him to the conclusion. New curricula must be constructed which will spark intuitive leaps in order that students will have practice in intuitive thinking while still in school. The pre-cognitive hunch is a kind of creative approach which must be nurtured and fostered as a vital part of the learning process. Associated with intuitive thinking is the discovery approach, which encourages each student to learn the subject in his own way. This technique is basic to modern theories of independent learning and creative thinking. The *discovery method* need not be so slow that the student must rediscover all that man has already learned. The subject matter must contain "built in" short cuts in the form of ideas introduced at regular intervals. They must be intermingled with cross-discussions among peers so that the individual will not be isolated from the discoveries and ideas of fellow students.

Time Variations in Curricula

The multiphased curriculum, in effect, is a process of educational change and all that this liberates in new ideas. This means that new materials should be based on different premises from those of the past. For example, the time element in which a student studies a given subject should be increasingly variable, and subject matter must cease to come only in one-year packages. Education may prove to be much more effective when subject matter can be divided into a variety of calendar systems including the quinary, the quarter and the multimester.

What are some of the possibilities when schools discontinue the old practice of dividing courses into segments one school year in length? Course matter can be much more relevantly divided into six-week units, seven-week units, nine-week units, or even eighteen-week units, especially when different teachers are assigned to the differing units. For example, consider the subject which is conventionally known as 10th grade English. In this subject the four major blocks of subject matter studied are the novel, the short story, the drama, and poetry. In large conventional schools, four or more teachers will each teach the whole year of 10th grade English. Instead, one teacher should teach poetry for the entire year, one the novel, one the short story, and one the drama. Students will, of course, change teachers ever nine weeks instead of once a year.

The variation allows the school to take advantage of two very important principles. First, this spreads talented teachers among all students; secondly, it spreads the poorer teachers as well. When one teacher teaches a certain course for an entire year, and a student is assigned to an incompetent teacher, he loses a year of work. With more frequent variation of teachers he would lose only a few weeks. It is just as appropriate to divide other subject matter on the same kind of basis. Consider the school which has four teachers handling American history. Instead of each teacher having to teach the whole course, one teacher can teach the concept of liberty as a nine-week unit, one the principles of equality for nine weeks, while the other two are teaching nine-week units on Communism and self-government. Students can be assigned to a different teacher for each nine-week unit. In the new framework of time and teacher variation, the idea of the "spiral curriculum" takes on new dimensions. The "spiral" is based on the theory that the major themes of a subject arise at different times and with increasing degrees of rigor and complexity. The flexibility of courses planned in shorter units and around major principles will give increased thrust to the development of "spiral curricula."

Phased Learning and Appropriate Placement

The major purpose of Appropriate Placement is to provide a school setting in which each student may proceed through a twelve-year learning sequence at the pace commensurate with his learning ability, unhampered by artificial and arbitrary pace-restrictions imposed upon him. Consequently, the primary advantage of suitable placement depends on the availability of accurate and reliable data on each student's learning ability. The system of phasing the curriculum by depth of learning is the means by which Appropriate Placement based on individual needs and capacities is implemented. It provides an easy vehicle by which the curriculum of each student can be kept in motion.

Desiderata

The purpose of education is to prepare individuals to make wise choices. Each student is afforded the opportunity to consider and arrive at important decisions vitally affecting his future in the revolutionary new Appropriate Placement school. Before registering, each student is encouraged to study carefully the school's organization and programs of studies, and to phase himself in line with his past achievement and present resolve. The school's staff should urge that no student enroll in courses phased below his intellectual potential, but this is a student's prerogative and responsibility—only the individual suffers from the consequences of not having been educated to his maximum potential.

One of the great mistakes that students make is to think of education only in terms of formal schooling. Each student is encouraged to regard learning as a process which begins at birth and ends only with death and is by no means limited to the classroom. In keeping with this philosophy, students enrolled in the Appropriate Placement school will find the library and laboratories open longer than in most schools. Furthermore, private arrangements should be made for responsible students working on special projects to gain access to the creative art or science laboratories even beyond the late afternoon and evening hours when these facilities are generally available.

Chapter Three

SCHOOL BUILDINGS FOR
PHASED CURRICULA

The question which comes to mind at this point is that of facilities and administration. Are unique facilities needed to operate a school in which the curriculum is built largely around individual learning? I am tempted to answer *no*, but this is not quite the case. Unique facilities are needed, but they are not so unusual as to require a new design of the school plant. The trick is to alter the existing building to suit the needs of the new program.

In the elementary school several rooms should be selected which are separated by non-load-bearing walls. These walls should be removed to provide a large space which can be furnished with carrels or similar private student work spaces. Activities which will take place in this environment are individualized and vary with the interest and talent of the individual. Some students will be reading, others will be drawing, and some may be engaged with programmed learning materials. Convenient listening booths equipped for recording, viewing, and listening should be ringed about the room.

The other types of space needed are numerous small areas which can be used for seminars and small group discussions. These can be constructed by partitioning some of the conventional classrooms into smaller areas. The result will be, instead of a school with all middle-sized space, a school made up of large space, small space and middle space.

The same formula applies to the nongraded junior high school plant. This school may, however, lend itself to more sweeping renovation. For example, if typing is offered, a sufficient number of walls should be removed to accommodate at least 100 typewriters. It is both uneconomical and inefficient to teach typing in groups of only 30 or 40 students. Drafting and drawing, like typing, can be taught in groups of 100 or more, so considerably more large space is needed in the junior high school. The purpose of large groups in typing and drawing, taught by just one teacher, is to provide flexibility of staff.

The senior high school plant should be altered along the same lines as the elementary and junior high. All levels of instruction in the nongraded school must center around varied space for a varied curriculum. The ultimate intent is for the carrel to serve as the student's home base.

A New Design for School Plants

While humble alterations are all that is required for a conventionally constructed school, the school plant which has not yet been built can and should become a monument to originality.

Space spectaculars have contributed greatly to the fostering of a national mood disposed to embracing boldly advanced concepts in the schools. The issue that confronts the architects of new schools today is simply this—do they dare take advantage of the national congeniality toward change and attempt advances in school buildings comparable to achievements in space? The environment for unorthodoxy in school plants is a contemporary social and industrial scene vigorously propelled by rapid and ever-accelerating change. In this setting the challenge to architects is to design buildings which will be appropriate in a rapidly changing educational system.

The effect of burgeoning space technology has been to make education all the rage, and experimentation has become acceptable in this traditionally conventional enterprise. Innovations such as the nongraded school are making drastic changes in the educational establishment. Imaginative teachers are teasing out the principal ideas from conventional subject matter, creating an exciting new climate for learning. Increasing numbers of students are assuming responsibility for their own learning, and the implications for a new process of education are simply enormous. Education will range from auto mechanics to thrust dynamics, from terrestrial geography to the topography of interstellar space, and the school plant itself must be so designed as to be capable of change and adaptation to serve tomorrow's education as well as today's. *The job of the architect in the age of cybernation is to keep the building from getting in the way of the educational program.*

Change in the design of school buildings is basic to developing the potential for creative education. The conventional school building is so filled with archaic design that it is a monument to built-in inefficiency. It is designed around the housekeeping activities of the janitor and the heating plant, and the students are made to fit afterwards, sorted into space which we have called classrooms. Winston Churchill put it well when he said, "We shape our buildings and thereafter they shape us."

The traditional school structure, from a functional as well as an aesthetic viewpoint, has an aspect of grimness about it. Picasso's comments on creative design have tremendous implications for nongraded school architecture: [1]

> What a sad thing for a painter who loves blondes but denies himself the pleasure of putting them in his pictures because they don't go well with the basket of fruit.
>
> What misery for a painter who detests apples to have to use them all the time because they harmonize with the tablecloth! I put in my picture everything I like. So much the worse for the things—they have to get along with one another.

We are badly in need of some school architecture which mixes a few blondes with the fruit. Still-life need not be bland, and we cannot afford conventional buildings in an unconventional age.

Traditionally, when a school system employs an architect to design a new school the first order of business is to concentrate on classrooms, their number, size, and shape. In the era of the nongraded school we should abandon the conventional classroom. The epoch of chambered education is passing as the schools move away from fellowship toward scholarship.

The New School Library

The architect should first turn his attention to the school library, and I am not talking here about the conventional library which exists in schools today. The new library must be as large as the gymnasium and as intensely used. Boards of Education must allocate as much money for books and materials of knowledge as they do for stadiums and physical education facilities. In the revamped concept of the library there should be a number of small soundproof rooms roughly six

---

[1] "Conversation with Picasso," *Cahiers D'Art* (Paris) 1935. Translated by Brewster Ghiselin in *The Creative Process*, New York, Mentor Books, 1952, p. 56.

feet square for typing, tape recorders, and other viewing and listening which may be connected with library research.

I would like to emphasize, however, that the important changes needed in education are principles, concepts, and methods. In accommodating these innovations we must beware of gimmicks and gadgets. So far, the chief target of the gadgeteers has been the school library. Among the mechanical contrivances being advocated are closed-circuit television, strato-vision, analog and digital computers, and a host of retrieval gimmicks. The fundamental need for libraries is books, and taxpayers can legitimately question the wisdom of investing large sums of money in electronic gadgetry when no competent materials have been developed to accompany the gadgets. What the schools need most are spacious libraries filled with books.

Carrels

The gradual disappearance of the need for constant teacher-student contact is bringing about the need for some kind of private work space for the student, and furniture for the nongraded school library must be designed so that every student will have visual as well as aural privacy. At first this will take the form of a movable carrel. The old idea of expecting students to concentrate and study, four and six to a table, is educational nonsense. The development of the carrel is the most important change in the seating and arrangement of students in the entire history of school furniture. Ever since the days of the bench manufacturers of school furniture have concentrated on unchildlike seating which has been of no help in the educational process.

The modern school building should be designed to accommodate vast numbers of both "dry" and "wet" carrels. (By "wet" carrels I mean carrels wired for electronics.) As the technology of education becomes more highly developed, more of the carrels would be "wet," but at the present time it would

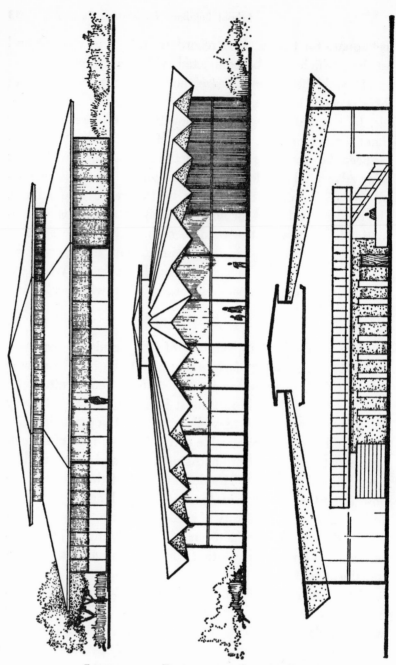

IMAGINATIVE DESIGNS FOR SCHOOL LIBRARIES

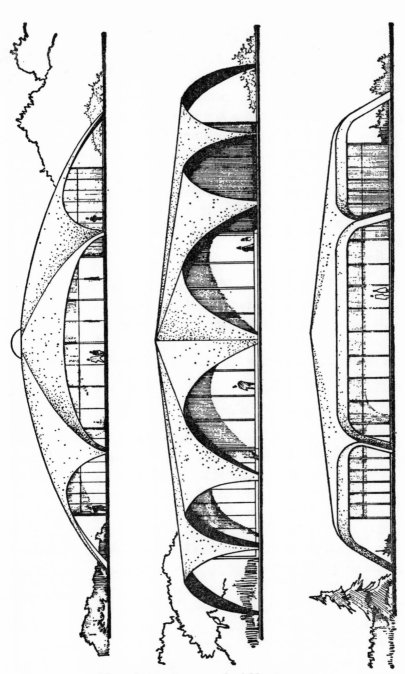

*These designs for new school libraries were
developed by Educational Facilities Laboratories.*

be wasteful to equip a school one hundred percent with electro-mechanically wired carrels since there are few good materials available for this use. The present need is for (1) many carrels which afford privacy as a home base for students, and (2) a number of small booths electro-mechanically wired for viewing, listening, and recording. While school furniture manufacturers are now beginning to produce an adequately designed carrel, little thought has been given so far to the design of a chair which is comfortable. It is important that students be comfortable both physically and mentally.

Librarians

In this new kind of library a new breed of librarian is needed. It must be her function above all to serve the students, sparing no effort to furnish them with the books they need and seeking every means to ignite their interest in others. The tasks of cataloging and censoring must be relegated to a position of far inferior importance.

A New Role for the Laboratory

After designing the library, the architect should next turn his attention to the laboratories. Sophisticated science laboratories, like the library, should be so designed that they can be used by the student in the afternoon and evening, with or without the teacher's presence. These new approaches defy conventional school buildings.

The language laboratory has become obsolete in five short years. In place of the language laboratory, the need is for an electro-mechanical laboratory serving many different disciplines. Such a multipurpose installation would accommodate the study not just of foreign language, but also of speech, shorthand, music appreciation, and other subjects which lend themselves to electro-mechanical teaching aids, all going on at the same time.

Zones of Space

At last, we come to the classroom. In the nongraded school, with youngsters taking more responsibility for their own education, it is no longer appropriate to group students in classrooms, thirty to the class. The space for discussion and lecturing should accommodate students sometimes in groups of five and sometimes in groups of a hundred or more. Space in the modern school must be sufficiently softened acoustically so that few walls are needed. The school arranged for flexibility will replace the classroom with intervals of space. In these differing space spheres teachers will meet with students in groups of varying size. Furthermore, students will be seated in diversified kinds of furniture depending on the nature of the subject; e.g., trapazoidal tables for history, where frequent discussions are taking place; individual carrels for mathematics, where independent study is the order of the day.

Once we have shifted from the school to the student the responsibility for his own learning, increasing numbers of students will receive their education by appointment, working most of the time on their own in independent study. This means that the only rigid space in the school plant should be the individual carrels for study. The rest of the physical plant will consist of flexible zones.

School Plant Accessibility

Another significant development which demands radical building changes is the recent discovery by the schools of the slow learners. Unfortunately, schools in the past have been neither deeply nor sincerely interested in slow learners, and only lately have they become embarrassed over the national drop-out rate, which now exceeds 30 percent of all high school youth. The United States, in its age of enlightenment, can no longer afford this continual drain on its potential. The only solution lies in the inauguration of special programs specifically planned to accommodate reluctant and hesitant learners. This means that the new design of school buildings must contain special laboratories equipped for "involvement" learning, deliberately designed to deal with about 40 percent of the students.

For the past ten years we have talked continuously about the flexibility of schools. We should now turn our attention to another link, one which has been missing for a long time: greater access to the creative components of the school plants. By creative elements, I mean the library, the art labs, the science labs, the electro-mechanical laboratory, and zones of space for lectures and discussions. Why do we need increased access to the school plant? With the tremendous explosions of new knowledge, six and a half hours a day is no longer sufficient time for the learning needs of either the student or the adult population. Both groups need to gain access to the school plant after regular hours. Consequently, the accent on the design of school buildings in the late nineteen sixties must center on the concept of a school open and available after school and in the evening.

If this chapter hasn't been imaginative enough about the school of tomorrow, I shall just mention a recent prediction by Harold Gores, President of Educational Facilities Laboratories of the Ford Foundation. Dr. Gores asserted that, at some future date, we may be squirting school buildings out of push-button cans. This may sound fantastic, but there was recently on exhibition in Washington, D. C., a building 30 feet wide which came out of a 50-gallon drum. This building was of course made of plastic, but if a building can come from a 50-gallon drum in 1965, why not from a push-button can in 1975?

Chapter Four

THE MULTIPHASED
PRIMARY SCHOOL

There is a charming story about the pre-school-age youngster who impatiently stayed home with his mother while four older brothers and sisters went to school. At last he became of age and the great day came for him to enter school. The youngster left home eagerly the first morning, anxious to enter the world of adventure about which he had heard so much for so long. After his first day at school he was asked at dinner what he thought of school. His reply contained a world of wisdom. "Oh," the youngster replied, "school is not such a much." School, indeed, has not been nearly enough for many youngsters. The mass movement of students through twelve grades of school has become one of the most chaotic in the history of mass movements. Soon after entering school, the individual student becomes lost in collective grouping and only rarely afterward does he have an opportunity to give expression to his individuality.

The Age Criterion

The whole process of education gets off to a bad start with the practice of admitting children into the first grade when they are six years old. The use of a non-intellective factor such as age to determine when a child will enter school sets the stage for inflexible education and conformity. The system used in Siam, where a child cannot start school until he can reach across the top of his head with his right arm and touch the lobe of his left ear, is as sensible as using the age of the child to determine when he is ready for school.

One of the chief reasons for today's stormy educational climate is the failure of educational researchers to uncover techniques for predicting the ability of students to do school work on the basis of evidence other than age. In the era of laser technology and lunar exploration the schools urgently need to discover how to forecast the kind of education which will best serve each individual. Until the mission of "how best to develop the intellect" is accomplished, we will be unable to prevent the extreme emotional wear and tear on young children which results from the arbitrary practice of putting all children in school when they are six years old.

The national picture regarding when a child should enter school is confusing. Each state has its own legislation governing the age that a child must reach before he can enter school, and state laws vary widely and indifferently. The unfortunate part of the problem lies in the fact that laws regarding age of admission to school were established in an era of residential stability.

We are now living in an age of mobility. In the nineteen sixties it is not unusual for an individual born in New York to attend elementary school in California, junior high school in Illinois and senior high in Florida.

One of the most controversial of the rules governing admission into the primary school is the cut-off date for starting to school. For example, in a certain northern state a student must be six years of age before November 30th of the year in which he enters school. Youngsters born on November 29th are eligible for admission. Those born two days later on December 1 must loiter an entire year before being eligible. Parents of bright children who are required to delay an extra year before entering a child invariably clash with the school system. In one high socio-economic residential area, where there is a predominance of parents with bright children, the school system recently discovered, entirely by accident, that a sizable number of frustrated parents had forged the birth certificates of their children in order to enter them in school ahead of time. Subsequent checking with the Bureau of Vital Statistics for the correct ages of all the children in the school revealed that, over the years, dozens of students had been entering school before reaching the legal school age. Changing the birth certificates had become a common practice. The most surprising part of the incident was the discovery that invariably the "illegally entered students" had done well in school work. Forging birth certificates cannot be condoned, but the success of these children indicates that a serious ambiguity exists in the practice of using age as the standard for admission to school.

Alternative Criteria for Admitting Students to School

So far as age is concerned, some children are ready to begin school when they are four years old. Others are not equipped to cope with the educational process when they have reached their sixth birthday. While the age of the child is an extremely unsatisfactory index for determining when the child will enter school, what are the alternative criteria for admitting children into the first grade?

1. Sex (have girls begin a year earlier than boys).
2. The Intelligence Quotient.
3. The amount of education of the child's parents.
4. The occupation of the child's parents.
5. A reading aptitude test.

None of these criteria constitutes an acceptable index of child-preparedness for schoolwork. What is badly needed to solve the dilemma of when a child should begin school is a newly designed verbal achievement test. Such an achievement test, based entirely on verbal factors, should not be difficult to construct. Commercial testing organizations such as the Educational Testing Service at Princeton or Science Research Associates, a subsidiary of I.B.M., could come up with such a test on very short notice if a demand should make itself known.

New Standards for Beginning School

Once a standard verbal achievement test has been conceived, all children should be tested on reaching their fifth birthday. The intent of these achievement tests is to determine at what stage in the learning process the student can be most appropriately started in school. Some youngsters will be able to move directly into the first grade when they are five years old, others should spend up to two years in a new kind of preparatory kindergarten. There is no reason why the kindergarten should be limited to one year. Many students can profitably spend two years preparing for a rigorous primary education. In the multiphased school of the future, age will be combined with social and intellective predictors to determine when a child enters school. The intent is to forecast the curriculum of the pre-school age child with the same precision which college admission officers now project college success.

Under this novel admissions plan, the curriculum of individual students will vary enormously. The extremes of this proposed arrangement are as follows:

MULTIPHASED KINDERGARTEN

Student A—whose verbal achievement is below the 30th percentile should spend two years in kindergarten.

Student B—whose verbal achievement is between the 30th and 50th percentiles need spend only one year in kindergarten.

Student C—whose verbal achievement is above the 50th percentile may enter directly into the primary school.

An interesting result of this plan is that the customary grade repeater will no longer need to repeat grades. He will, instead, spend up to two years becoming better prepared to undertake serious schoolwork. Provisions must be included for frequent evaluation of learning so that any student can move ahead whenever he is ready to do so.

Modern educational research gives strong support to the idea of admitting youngsters to school at an earlier age than the conventional sixth year. Henry Chauncey, President of Educational Testing Service reports:

> The implications are that intelligence is not completely fixed from birth, but is subject of considerable influence during the early years and to a lesser and lesser extent as the child matures. Second, that mental processes which become established very early in life become a permanent part of the individual and exert continuing effects upon his mental growth and educational development throughout his life.[1]

A firm advocate of earlier admission to school is the Superintendent of the Barrington, Illinois, schools, Robert M. Finley. Dr. Finley's plan is to send each child a card on his fifth birth-

---

[1] *Education U.S.A.*, January 23, 1964 (a publication of the National School Public Relations Associations, a Department of the National Education Association), Washington, D.C.

day saying "Happy Birthday! Come to School!" The school curriculum should be flexible enough to admit a child at any time of the year. And what a change in attitude may result on the part of both the pupils and the school if the privilege of starting to school comes as a birthday present!

The Nongraded Primary Structure

Perhaps the oldest continually operated nongraded primary and certainly the best known of them is the Milwaukee nongraded primary program. One of its mentors, supervisor Florence Kelly, reports that this program was first instituted in 1942 and has continued successfully ever since. The Milwaukee plan for a nongraded primary school must be given credit for establishing the pattern for the nation.

The organization of the nongraded primary school includes what are commonly known as grades one, two, and three. The nongraded process eliminates the requirement that a youngster spend a year in a class and has invented a process by which the youngster is given material in line with his achievement. The objective of this plan is to deal with individual differences, make progress more continuous, and release young children from the pressures and tensions of failure and needless grade repetition.

There are three basic principles which buttress the organization of the nongraded primary school:

1. Some youngsters complete the primary unit in two years and are assigned to the intermediate school at the end of their second year in school.
2. Some students spend four years in the ungraded primary and are placed in the intermediate school at the end of their fourth year in school.
3. No student is allowed to remain in the primary area more than four years. After that length of time an individual must be either assigned to retarded educable classes or entered in the intermediate school.

To allow a two-year separation of students by chronological age, almost from the time they enter school, is one of the strong features of the nongraded primary process. This is certainly superior to the graded school concept of social promotion. In graded schools when youngsters are socially promoted for physical or emotional reasons, the school still remains insensitive to their intellectual needs. The theory of continuous progress argues that all children are different and, while some will remain in the primary area longer than others, learning moves constantly forward for all. By comparison, the theory of graded education contends that all children must pass a fixed curriculum at each grade level; if they fail to do so, they must repeat all of the material studied. This is an affront to their intellectual development, since grade repeaters are required to repeat many things which they have already learned. It is ridiculous for a student to have to go through all of the work of an entire grade for a second time. This is a tremendous waste of his time and penalizes his intellectual development.

The plan of the nongraded primary school never demands that a child repeat what he has already learned, even when a youngster is required to spend extra time in the primary area before he enters the intermediate school. What the system is really doing is handling retention and acceleration in a more efficient and subtle fashion than in the conventionally graded primary school.

Basic Concepts of the Nongraded Primary

One of the major goals of the nongraded primary school is to decrease the wide range of abilities which the teacher of a particular group of youngsters is required to face. It has become apparent that the teacher can teach more efficiently if the youngsters in a particular class are of more nearly the same intellectual background. No one expects all youngsters to be at the same level of achievement, but an important concept of the nongraded primary is the narrowing of the spread of abilities in a particular class.

The Joplin Plan

One of the most provocative reading plans ever to be developed is the nongraded plan originated in the Joplin, Missouri, public schools. The success of this innovation has been remarkable. Succinctly stated, every child learns to read efficiently in Joplin. The "Joplin Plan" has created so much interest in the teaching profession that I have paraphrased a *Readers' Digest* report on this exciting development.

This is how the Joplin Plan works. When it's time for reading, the class—assuming it's a 4th grade—forgets it is a 4th grade class. The students break up into different groups and go to reading classes which vary from the 2nd all the way to the 9th grade level. Once the students have been re-assembled for reading they are associated with other students who are of different ages but who are at their own stage of reading development. Furthermore, they are allowed to advance as rapidly as they can. No student is frustrated by being behind the rest of the class and no one is bored by being ahead. Everybody succeeds.

Another interesting innovation in the Joplin Plan is that after the reading class is over the students are permitted to have a twenty-five minute free reading period. They may read anything they like. The only stipulation is that they enjoy what they are reading. The Joplin Plan has come to be widely known in educational circles as one of the easiest strategies for nongrading youngsters and regrouping them on the basis of reading achievement. The plan concentrates on grades 4, 5, and 6 where the age range is from 9 to 12. Joplin educators consider these the crucial years as far as reading is concerned.

This plan was launched in 1953 by the Joplin superintendent of schools, and since that time it has become widely used as the basic pattern for the nongraded reading program. The beauty of the plan is that it requires no new teachers and no more money except for a new and wider range of books to accommodate the learning differences of the students. And this holds true of the nongraded Appropriate Curriculum Placement Plan.

The Nongraded Curriculum

The curriculum of the Appropriate Placement primary school should not be forged solely around achievement in reading, but should also include achievement in mathematics. Beyond the primary, in the nongraded intermediate, the curriculum should be broadened even more and fashioned around achievement in the four basic areas of language arts, mathematics, science and social learning. In the years ahead, when we learn more about the margin between the quick and the slow, the nongraded primary will be forged around achievement in art, science and social learnings in addition to reading and mathematics.

The Nongraded Primary in Philadelphia

The Philadelphia plan for a nongraded primary system has been singled out as a model and will be explained in some detail. There are several reasons for using the Philadelphia plan as a model. The city has high national visibility. The migration in and out of Negroes from the segregated South has given it more than its share of the deprived and the segregated. These circumstances demonstrate the adaptability of nongradedness and focus on its potential as a solution to the problem of big cities which have become saturated by the culturally and economically deprived.

The educational leadership of Philadelphia has done such an excellent job of setting forth the guidelines for the nongraded primary operation that the Philadelphia program is clearly understood through excerpts from the school system's bulletins. The statement of the Philadelphia Public School Continuous Progress Primary Unit Committee contains the basic principles of the plan:

> These principles are fundamental to any consideration and development of this unit:
>
> A. Children vary in their rate of learning.
> B. Continuous progress for all children is a major objective.
> C. Pacing curriculum experience and instruction to the learner's rate of achievement is an essential of an effective program.
> D. Flexible organization to provide for periodic regrouping is needed to meet child growth and to further continuous progress.
> E. Reading achievement provides the best single criterion for grouping in the early school years.
> F. For grouping, it is necessary to make certain that all curriculum areas receive due emphasis and that the child's individual needs receive adequate attention.
> G. In any regrouping plan it is important that the young child be guarded against the impact of change by making certain that the school program provides experiences which will enable him to adjust as easily as possible to different personalities and surroundings.[2]

WHAT PRINCIPALS AND TEACHERS SHOULD DO

I. Before the end of June
   A. 1. In June administer the Philadelphia Verbal Ability Test, Kindergarten and Grade I, to those kindergarten pupils who will be assigned to the program of the first year in September.
   2. Transfer the I.Q. and Verbal score to the Cumulative Record.

---

[2] *"The Continuous Progress Primary Unit,"* A Preliminary Statement of the Philadelphia Public Schools. May, 1961.

3. Interpret the I.Q. and Verbal scores.
B. Secure the kindergarten teacher's evaluation of the relative pupil readiness for learning.
C. Set up a conference composed of the principal, kindergarten teachers, and teachers of the program of the first year to screen and assign pupils for initial grouping.
II. During September
A. Assign pupils who have not had Philadelphia kindergarten experience to initial groups on the basis of chronological age and any other available data indicative of their relative readiness.
B. 1. The second or third week in September administer the Philadelphia Verbal Ability Test, Kindergarten and Grade I, to those pupils to whom it has not been given previously.
2. Transfer the I.Q. and Verbal scores to the Cumulative Record.
3. Interpret the I.Q. and Verbal scores.
C. Continue to evaluate the relative readiness of all pupils, using all of the supportive information available, so that future refinement of grouping can be undertaken most effectively.[3]

The argument that the nongraded primary is ideally suited to high socio-economic communities but not appropriate to communities of the disadvantaged is vigorously refuted in Philadelphia.

The Nongraded Primary in Chicago

Further effectiveness of the nongraded primary as an organization well suited to the education of the deprived and segregated is illustrated by the results obtained in the Nikola Tesla school deep in the slums of Chicago. The imaginative principal of this school, Jerome Gilbert, describes the Nikola Tesla experiment as follows:

---

[3] *Ibid.*

"The nongraded program at Tesla is called the Continuous Development Program. It was instituted after a study of our school records revealed that nearly 32 percent of our students failed during their first three years in school.

"The Continuous Development Program seems the answer to a prayer in a school district such as ours, where many of the parents receive some form of public assistance, have relatively little education, and move frequently. Our program seeks to minimize these cultural factors by providing more time for children to orient themselves to the academic and social goals of the school in an atmosphere free from the twin threats of boredom and failure.

"Our teaching staff finds greater satisfaction in their teaching because they have the pleasure of seeing youngsters succeed." [4]

Superintendent Benjamin Willis of Chicago reports widespread interest among Chicago's elementary schools in the nongraded primary, and many other schools are following the leadership of Nikola Tesla.

Park Forest, Illinois, Nongraded Primary

In contrast to these plans is the one in Park Forest, Illinois, a community of middle-class people with numerous cultural advantages.

A unique feature for the Park Forest plan is the admissions age. At Park Forest automatic registration in school is permitted for all students who are six before September 1. Youngsters whose sixth birthday falls between September 1 and December 31 must be screened by a carefully designed testing program. When a youngster in this age bracket demonstrates extreme immaturity, his parents are requested to delay entering him in school until the next school year.

---

[4] *Report to the Seminar on the Deprived and the Segregated.* M.I.T. Endicott House, Dedham, Massachusetts, Sept., 1963.

Mobility of Students

In the Park Forest plan, when a child is about ready to move to another classroom he is given an introductory period of two weeks in which he is sent to the new classroom part of each day, usually for reading. This arrangement is expected to adjust him to the new group. Once he finds his new experiences pleasing and more satisfying, it is actually his desire and request that brings about the completion of his move.

Lincoln Sudbury Nongraded Primary

Another high socio-economic community with a successful nongraded primary school is Lincoln Sudbury, Massachusetts. Here transition teachers are used to assist students in adjusting to new situations. When a youngster is to be moved to another group he spends a certain amount of time with a transition teacher before moving. Progression through the nongraded primary is much like that of the graded school, except the stops and starts are gone. Some students complete the primary unit in two years, others take four.

School-Parent Communication

One of the first questions broached by educators who are considering introducing the nongraded primary in their communities is how to communicate with and obtain the co-operation of parents. The methods used in a number of school systems were compiled by K. C. Austin at the University of Colorado:

Means Used to Inform the Public About
Ungraded Primary Units

Parent-teacher conferences
School visitations by general public
General meetings during school year
"Open house" meetings at the schools

Bulletins sent home with children
Newspaper stories and publicity
Parent handbooks
Home visitations by school personnel
Citizens' planning and evaluation committees
Pre-school orientation meetings
Radio programs and publicity
School newspapers
Pre-school parent-teacher conferences
Television programs and publicity
Business-Education Week.[5]

A major concern of schools giving consideration to the nongraded primary plan is the kind of achievement tests to use in the re-grouping of students from gradedness to nongradedness. This matter was carefully researched by Austin and the results are as follows:

Standardized Academic Achievement Tests
Used in Ungraded Primary Schools

California Achievement
Tests accompanying reading series
Metropolitan Reading Readiness
Stanford Achievement
Metropolitan Achievement
Gates Primary Reading
Gates Reading Readiness
California Reading Readiness
Harrison Readiness
Iowa Every-Pupil
Lee Clark Reading Readiness.[6]

Reporting to Parents

There is absolutely no uniformity in the manner in which nongraded primaries evaluate pupils to indicate their progress.

---

[5] K. C. Austin, "The Ungraded Primary Unit in Public Elementary Schools of the United States" (Doctoral Thesis, University of Colorado, 1957), p. 121.
[6] *Ibid.*, p. 98.

In his study of marking practices in thirty-one nongraded primary schools Austin reported the following variations:

*Number of Times Per Year Pupil Progress
Reports Are Made to Parents*

Frequency of Reporting	Number of Schools
Six times yearly	10
Five times yearly	1
Four times yearly	14
Three times yearly	2
Two times yearly	3
One time yearly	1

In its detailed analysis the report adds:

> Twenty-nine, or about 94 percent, of the schools determined a pupil's progress, at least in part, by comparing what he did with what he was capable of doing according to his own indicated abilities. Ten of these schools said a child's progress report was based entirely upon comparison with his own abilities. Twelve schools reported progress of a child, in part, by comparison of achievement with national norms. Six said they compared children's achievement with others in their class group, while five indicated the child's progress was reported in terms of the school's own pre-determined standards.[7]

The N.E.A. and the Nongraded School

Until quite recently professional educational leadership organizations carefully avoided facing up to the wide variability of the differences in learning. Their reluctance stemmed from feelings of inadequacy over their inability to fashion a program of individual differences which could be easily administered. This attitude on the part of professional organizations is now undergoing a revolution. The recently published N.E.A. Project on Instruction, heralded as the most important instructional document since the statement of the "Seven Cardinal

---

[7] *Ibid.*, pp. 124–125.

Principles of Education" in 1918, contains the first major statement by a professional group of the extreme variability of individual differences:

> Learners vary widely in their school achievement. The spread in average achievement in an elementary school class slightly exceeds the number of the grade level. That is, this spread in achievement is more than three years in a third grade class, four in a fourth grade, five in a fifth grade, and so on. By the junior high school years, this over-all spread is estimated to be approximately two thirds the mean average of the grade group. A group entering the seventh grade is approximately twelve years of age. Two thirds of 12 is 8. Consequently, the spread in achievement is from the third grade to the eleventh.[8]

Educational leaders have long recognized that children differ physically, socially, and emotionally, but they have paid only lip service to intellectual differences. At long last, recognition is about to be given to the area which contains the greatest difference of all—variance in intellectual powers.

Conclusions About the Nongraded Primary

The major drawback to the nongraded primary lies in the over-emphasis currently being placed on non-essentials. Not nearly enough attention has been given to the development of a high-powered curriculum to go with the dynamics of the structure. The program of studies for the nongraded primary seems hopelessly bogged down as its proponents concentrate on new terminology more than anything else. For instance, almost all of the descriptions of nongraded primary programs begin with this kind of sentence: "No longer do we use the term grade in our school system." This statement is usually followed by a description of new educational phraseology.

---

[8] *Planning and Organizing for Teaching* (Washington, D.C., The National Education Association, 1963), p. 13.

The second big worry of nongraded primary teachers has centered on the matter of what kinds of records to keep. If half of the energy spent on developing jargon and new records had been directed toward a new program, the movement would indeed be much farther along. This kind of absurdity was epitomized in one school system which developed and issued new records even before the teachers understood what the nongraded program was all about.

Where should the nongraded primary go from here? Consideration should be given to a refinement of the process by which students are phased into subjects. They should also be phased in subjects other than reading and arithmetic. A more refined grouping in art, social studies and science may add much greater flexibility to this process. Secondly, the primary school must put increasing pressure on the intermediate school to nongrade its curriculum also. If continuous progress in individually styled learning is good for primary school age youngsters, it is equally appropriate for the later elementary school.

The nongraded school is a proven process of teaching which is here to stay. The U.S. Office of Education reports that 20 percent of all primary schools have some involvement in it, yet with all of its imaginative potential it has limped along for twenty-five years without making much of a dent in the educational establishment. Its growth and development have been constrained by two major barriers. First, the nongraded primary has not been innovative enough to comprise a notable change. Its curriculum has maintained most of the conventions of the graded schools and its ungradedness has consisted mostly of ungraded reading programs. With the exception of reading, the rest of the primary studies have remained graded. Actually, even the reading program of the nongraded primary has not been completely unpackaged. For example, while visiting a nongraded primary in California recently, I asked a teacher of six-year-olds how far ahead a bright youngster could range in reading. She replied that she would not let anyone go beyond the second grade reader for fear that they might get too far ahead of the class. It is this attitude of caution and restraint on the part of primary school teachers that has constrained the nongraded primary.

The second limitation on the development of a real break-through at the primary level is the fact that the intermediate grades constitute the superstructure of the elementary school. Their rigidity has stultified progress and created a major stumbling block to the full development of the ungraded primary.

Harold G. Shane describes the need well:

> At present, in our elementary schools, there is a long-standing need to act more constructively with regard to the problem of how best to help children progress through the grades. Some applied common sense and a good-sized dash of imagination are in order if we are to resolve the promotion-policy dilemma.[9]

The presently developed ungraded primary is in the unique position of being widely recommended but seldom adopted. Even when it is adopted it is often badly used. It has simply failed to espouse a bold enough structure.

Supervisor Florence Kelly of the Milwaukee system, writing for the professional magazine *Childhood Education,* described the nongraded program as "not a method of teaching but rather an administrative technique."[10] This points up sharply the difference in the kind of nongraded primary which I am advocating and the program which currently exists in most ungraded primary schools. The nongraded school is positively not an administrative technique, nor is it "just

---

[9] "Promotion Policy Dilemma." *National Education Association Journal,* 42:411, October, 1953.

[10] F. C. Kelly, "The Primary School in Milwaukee," *Childhood Education,* 24:236, January, 1948.

a change in organization." In the nongraded school the organization is changed for the specific purpose of coupling the material that the individual is expected to learn with his already acquired knowledge. Nongradedness is not concerned with its effect upon either the *administration* or the *organization*. Its major interest is in the *individual and his differences*.

Far too much emphasis has been placed on the organization and administration of the nongraded primary unit and not nearly enough attention paid to the curriculum. Actually, the organization and administration are the least consequential parts. Their function is largely housekeeping. The curriculum is the intellectual component.

The Curriculum for the Multiphased Primary School

The curriculum is a continuum with students grouped by achievement.

> Phase 1—Students who are achieving between 0 and the 10th percentiles. (These students must spend most of the school day studying reading, speaking and listening.) Music and art should be integrated into the program.
>
> Phase 2—Students who are achieving between the 10th and 25th percentiles. (These students spend a considerable part of the school day studying reading, speaking and listening.) Music, art and some mathematics should be integrated into the program.
>
> Phase 3—Students who are achieving between the 25th and the 45th percentiles. (These students also concentrate heavily on reading but less than students in phases 1 and 2.) Music, art and more mathematics should be integrated into the program.
>
> Phase 4—Students who are achieving between the 45th and the 70th percentiles. (These students spend only a normal amount of time in reading, listening and speaking and begin to delve seriously into science,

social studies and mathematics.) Music and art
should be integrated into the program.
Phase 5—Students who are achieving above the 70th per-
tile. (These students can range broadly in their
studies and can spend considerable time studying
mathematics, science and social studies.) Music and
art are included.

The nongraded school with its phased curriculum was
launched on the premise that students vary enormously in their
achievement. This variance is notable when youngsters first
enter school but the spread increases dramatically with each
succeeding year. By the time a group of students who started
in the first grade together reach the seventh grade, the spread
of achievement in every subject will vary from the second grade
all the way up to the freshman college level. But we must not
wait until youngsters have been in school many years to meet
their differences. We must meet them at every level of learning
and in every learning situation. This approach has enormous
implications for the Appropriate Placement primary school.

New Curricula for the Primary Division

The new flexible curricula for the Appropriate Placement
primary school should be developed around units rather than a
rigid year-long curriculum. The intent of the finished product
is to: (1) let each unit develop in its own way and not in
accordance with a preconceived pattern; (2) have curricula
materials built around phenomena which children observe—
not around definitions, dates, and rules; (3) develop a variety
of simple materials and techniques that involve children in
experimentation which they can pursue at their own pace and
describe in their own terms; (4) devise inexpensive curricular
equipment and familiar hardware which students can handle
easily in their individual carrels.

Chapter Five

THE MULTIPHASED
INTERMEDIATE SCHOOL

The area of learning known as the intermediate school has become an educational quagmire. For one thing, teaching in this division of the elementary school has too long been dominated by authoritarianism. Intermediate school pedagogy dogmatically emphasizes factual knowledge rather than conceptual knowledge. The business of the intermediate classroom revolves around a "question and answer" routine: the teacher often asks trite and uninteresting questions to which she expects pat and often stereotyped answers. This is not *always* the case, but I think if the reader examines his own experience, he will agree that this is *often* the case. The whole process was aptly described recently by an intermediate age youngster who remarked sadly that his teacher was "too busy giving answers to questions that nobody asked."

A less amusing practice is the custom which many intermediate school teachers have of rejecting incorrect answers in a manner calculated to be embarrassing to the student. David Paige, one of the nation's brightest and most creative teachers of intermediate arithmetic, believes that there should be no such thing as a "wrong" answer for students at this level of learning. In his classroom, Paige treats an erroneous reply as the right answer to the wrong question. *He then poses the question to fit the answer which was given.*

Equally ineffectual as the practice of embarrassing the pupil whose answer is wrong, is the habitual action of discarding answers that contain an element of truth but which are not quite the answer the teacher wants. As a scheme of learning, the authoritarian question and answer practices used in the intermediate school frustrate rather than teach. In this stultifying atmosphere, a passive situation has arisen from which the student is anxious to escape. Most teachers in the intermediate school have assumed too much responsibility for the learner's development. They have not permitted the student to develop independently, nor have they allowed him to exercise any degree of control over his activities in the learning process. Their role has been one of over-direction. The trend has been to make students passive.

Students should not be required to dissipate their energies on trivial pursuits. They must be allowed to feel a strong sense of involvement in, and identification with, their curriculum. In short, the teaching in most intermediate schools offers only the thinnest variety of intellectual nourishment. To a child, the intermediate school is often little more than a bureaucratic routine.

In deploring this state of affairs, Professor Jerome Wiesner, formerly President Kennedy's Chief Science Advisor, points out that recent startling discoveries about the capacities of the young for learning have not been incorporated into the teaching process. According to Wiesner, "the schools can teach more things earlier when they teach a subject right the first time. The student may come to understand it better later, but he does not have to discard what he has already learned."

Preserving the Status Quo

Innovators attempting to revamp the intermediate school must recognize that the consequences of their efforts will resemble the situation described by the nineteenth century Irishman, William Carleton, who once wrote:

> We argued the thing at breakfast, we argued the thing at tea. And the more we argued the question, the more we didn't agree.

But already we have waited too long for entrenched interests to agree. Further delay in the effort to revitalize this sadly neglected area may well be calamitous.

The intermediate school has not only restrained innovation in its own bailiwick; it has hampered nongradedness in the primary school. The unwillingness of the intermediate teaching staff to accommodate individual differences through nongrading has condemned the nongraded primary school to a kind of cloistered detachment. The intermediate school must no longer ignore the margin between the quick and the slow. It must recognize and accommodate the enormous spread of achievement which exists among its students.

The elementary schools do an adequate job for the gifted student largely because their parents are outspoken and critical. The parents of reluctant learners, on the other hand, are often from low socio-economic backgrounds and neither represent a political entity or express a very active concern for their children. The result is that children of low socio-economic standing are often sacrificed to the schools' weaker teachers, while superior students are funneled into classes taught by the schools' more able teaching staffs. This very process of discriminatory teacher assignment is the first seeding of the dropout problem.

A Tailor-made Curriculum

The educational system has failed to pay much attention to the improvement of individuals; its efforts have been directed toward improvement of the mass. In an era which Charles E. Silberman, writing for *Fortune* magazine, describes as the growing need for "masses of intellectuals," . . . the shift must be made to a mass attempt to improve the individual.

One of the most vigorous of the spokesmen calling for a school system which recognizes and plans for individual needs is Don H. Parker. Dr. Parker writes:

> We seem to have no trouble at all in accepting individual differences in the world of grown-ups, yet we consistently behave toward children and their education as though they were all alike.
>
> When, during the schooling process, they turn up with differences in learning ability, we actually become distressed!
>
> We seem able to ignore individual differences in schooling while adjusting to and providing for them in business and industry, as well as in the necessities of life.
>
> How did it come about—this almost incredible condition of apparently ignoring individual differences among children, especially in learning ability? [1]

Mediocrity in the intermediate school is basically the fault of the curriculum, which has failed to take into account the

---

[1] *Schooling for Individual Excellence.* (New York: Thomas Nelson and Sons, 1963), p. 90.

intellectual differences between boys and girls. Two and even three times as many boys as girls are low achievers. Girls have marked superiority over boys in areas such as reading comprehension, language arts, spelling, and foreign languages, yet no attempt has been made to accommodate this disparity. The intermediate school passes along entirely too many male students without teaching them properly. The result is that many boys are able but unproductive students.

No longer should there be a curriculum for the school or the grade. On the contrary, there must be a curriculum for each individual in the school. Take, for example, a student who is capable of doing seventh grade mathematics: he may be reading at only the third grade level while he may have a fourth grade knowledge of science and the talent of a fifth grader in art. If, rather than all ten-year-old youngsters being in the fifth grade, they spent their day being taught at the level of their achievement by various teachers, the curriculum of each individual would reflect these factors of achievement. His course of study would be so constructed that he would receive special instruction in reading in a small class, and would be scheduled for extra time in this subject.

In the words of Yale University's former child-development specialist, Dr. Arnold Gesell, "Each child travels by his own tailor-made schedule." This is an apt description of the central objective in the multiphasing. The purpose of a nongraded school is to permit ideas to be fed at the student's level of achievement. The most distinctive idea in the Appropriate Placement school is that students are respected as individuals, whether they are geniuses or slow learners, and efforts are made to fit them and their studies together. Students are not all cut to the same pattern—they have different interests, think differently, grow differently, and therefore need individually tailored programs. A personalized curriculum strives to place each of its students in the appropriate phase in each subject, and is always open to change if it seems in the best interest of the student.

The Elementary Principal

One cause of the crisis in the middle grades is the conformity which is sustained by the elementary school principal. The administrators of elementary schools invariably assume roles in which they perform clerical routine duties. Rarely do they undertake educational leadership. Croft Educational Services, in their "Executive Action Letter," reported recently that modern research has concluded that elementary principals do not initiate change. In fact, most current research indicates that they may even be biased against innovation and change. It is sad that one of the major obstacles to improvement in the middle grades is the attitude of the principal himself. Father Kulkin, Director of the Communication Arts Center at Fordham University, concluded a letter to me recently with these words: "Remember the administrator's prayer, *Ne Sim* Obex." [2] How comforting it would be if a few public elementary school principals could be persuaded to Father Kulkin's philosophy!

Required Course of Study

The growing emphasis on science and technology needs to be counterbalanced if we are to remain a sane and stable society, and the best possible way to do this is through a vigorous liberal arts program in the public high schools. Preparation for this must be in the intermediate schools, in the rigorous teaching of the fundamentals. In the multiphased intermediate school, the language arts, which include reading and writing, are considered to be the most important subjects in the curriculum. Approximately one third of the school day must be

---

[2] May I not be an obstacle.

scheduled for this fundamental area. Second in importance is mathematics. The language arts and mathematics should occupy fully fifty percent of the time spent in the school program. A complete breakdown of the amount of time which should be spent in each required area is as follows:

*Percentage of Time in Each Subject in
the Multiphased Intermediate School*

Language Arts	30%
Mathematics	20%
Science	15%
History and Social Sciences ...	15%
Art and Music	10%
Physical Education	10%

Total 100%

Varying Phases by Subjects

In the middle grades of the elementary school the phasing process assumes a unique design. Here the flexibility of phasing comes into full play when it provides a varying curriculum for the small school constructed to accommodate only a few students. Where the student population of the middle grades is limited, the phased process takes on a more flexible posture, for the grouping is varied not only with the needs of the youngster but also with the importance of the subject matter. The result is that in the more important basic subjects there will be several phases, while in the less important subjects there may be only two or three. This variation in the number of phases in a subject is essential when the middle grades in the elementary school do not have a large enough student capacity to "full phase" every subject.

The average elementary school accommodates only 600 students. This means that the middle grades contain approximately 300 students. In a typical traditionally graded organization a student population of 300 would be distributed somewhat as follows:

4 fourth grade classes
3 fifth grade classes
3 sixth grade classes

No grouping arrangement within the grade will give the flexibility needed to really link the curriculum to the achievement of the student. I call the new notion of varying the phases of the different subjects *multiformed phasing*. It is also called network phasing and cobweb phasing, the latter because the curriculum design becomes as complex and intricate as a spider's web.

Multiformed Phasing in the Language Arts

Since reading, listening, and speaking are the most important skills to be learned, the curriculum of the language arts must be the most carefully tailored to the individual's needs. As a consequence the language arts program is more finely phased.

Curriculum Phase 1 . . . A program is planned for students who need remedial assistance in small classes. The achievement level of these youngsters lies between 0 and the 20th percentile.

Curriculum Phase 2 . . . The curriculum is arranged for students who are weak in the basic skills. The intent of the curriculum here is to strengthen basic skills. The achievement of these students lies between the 20th and the 40th percentiles.

Curriculum Phase 3 . . . The curriculum for these youngsters must be geared to the average, or nearly so. The achievement of youngsters in this phase is between the 40th and the 70th percentiles.

Curriculum Phase 4 . . . The curriculum for these youngsters must be extensive. Here are youngsters who are capable of learning in depth. Their achievement is between the 70th and the 90th percentiles.

Curriculum Phase 5 . . . The curriculum for the academically able must be open ended and these youngsters must be allowed the freedom to range far ahead of their classmates. Their achievement is above the 90th percentile.

Note that it is important to keep the range narrower among the more modest learners, because their learning gap handicaps their performance. The range is also restricted for the very bright but for a different reason: very few students fall into this category, and much of their work may be done independently.

Multiformed Phasing in Mathematics

After the language arts the most important subject in the middle grades is mathematics. Like the language arts this subject should be taught in at least four phases whenever the student population permits.

Curriculum Phase 1 . . . The mathematics program for these students should be remedial and the classes small. Their achievement level should be from 0 to the 20th percentile.

Curriculum Phase 2 . . . The mathematics program for these students should provide for basic and average learning. Their achievement should range from the 20th to the 40th percentiles.

Curriculum Phase 3 . . . The mathematics curriculum for these students should be average and above. The achievement level

> of these youngsters should fall between the 40th and the 70th percentiles.
>
> Curriculum Phase 4 . . . The curriculum at this level should be planned for able and talented students. The achievement of these students should be above the 70th percentile.

Multiformed Phasing in Science

Science is a very important subject. However, it is neither as important as language arts nor as basic as the mathematical skills. For this reason, when the student population requires a curtailment in the number of phases or divisions, science is a likely place to truncate.

> Curriculum Phase 1 . . . This curriculum is designed for the youngster who has acquired little knowledge of science. Students in this phase are achieving between 0 and the 30th percentile.
>
> Curriculum Phase 2 . . . This curriculum is planned for youngsters who learn science in an average way. Students in this program are achieving between the 30th and the 65th percentiles.
>
> Curriculum Phase 3 . . . This curriculum is arranged for students with proven achievement and interest in science. Achievement is between the 65th and 99th percentiles

Multiformed Phasing in Social Studies

Social studies is an area where the minimum number of phases can be operated. For one thing the social studies as taught in the schools are not as important as the language arts, mathematics and science. Secondly, the structure of social learnings is such that this subject is more adaptable to heterogeneity than the other basic subjects.

Curriculum Phase 1 . . . A curriculum planned for young-
                                    sters who are below average in their
                                    basic knowledge of social science.

Curriculum Phase 2 . . . A curriculum organized for students
                                    who are average or above in their
                                    understandings of the subject.

The multiformed phasing described here is a model show-
ing extreme variations. The process can be as varied as the
student population and their needs indicate. In large elementary schools it will be possible to "full phase" every subject.
In smaller schools the important subjects may be finely phased
and the less important may be more broadly phased. Under the
principles of the Appropriate Placement plan the intermediate
school must focus sharply on the matter of increased numbers
of students learning independently and individually. With a
little ingenius engineering of the learning situation, remarkable
results can be achieved.

The elementary schools have been operating on the assumption that as age increases the length of time in private
study can increase proportionately. This does not necessarily
follow. I have seen very young primary students in the Mon-
tessori schools of Holland working individually for long
stretches of time. *The factor here is the task which the student
is performing rather than the age of the student.* The schools
must dismiss the old-fashioned idea that the older you are
the better you are. Both age and status must be "designed out"
of the curriculum.

THE SUMMERHILL SCHOOL

The intermediate school of the future lies somewhere
between the conventional school and the radical approach to
child rearing and learning which is advocated by the Summerhill School in Summerhill, England. After a lengthy visit to
Summerhill, I came away with the impression that here indeed

is one of the most unusual schools in the world. Some of its revolutionary nongraded activities have implications for all schools.

I cannot endorse the Summerhill practice of not compelling children to go to class, but I do strongly recommend the Summerhill approach to learning when they do attend class. The Summerhill notion of education is that of a nongraded curriculum geared both to the capacities of the youngsters and to their psychic needs. The major objective of the program is for youngsters to learn to face the world as individuals, grasping it intellectually, emotionally, and artistically. In essence, the philosophy of Summerhill is that intellectual development itself is not enough. Education must be emotional as well as intellectual, on the premise that there is no separation between intellect and feeling, and man's expression must not be limited to expressions of thought but also include his sensory perceptions.

The Gattegno and Cuisenaire Approach

After studying the philosophy of Summerhill with its emotional and intellectual emphasis, I feel that despite its promise, it lacks the imaginative twist espoused by other leading European educators including Cuisenaire and Gattegno. If school programs are to exhibit refreshment and renewal strength, a greater emphasis must be placed on the development of new patterns of thinking. This is the promise of Gattegno.

Learning in the multiphased intermediate school follows the Gattegno idea that teaching must be subordinated to learning. The best learning comes from asking good questions. Therefore, the teacher's first concern must be that of arousing curiosity. The new emphasis is on student information-getting rather than on teacher information-giving, where, unfortunately, there has been too little emphasis in the past. Students must be taught to think, to trust their intuitions, to make shrewd guesses, to develop brave hypotheses, and to respond with sound conclusions. The elementary schools have not been making an adequate effort in this area.

Dr. Caleb Gattegno may well have produced the first materials and techniques that subordinate teaching to learning. Much of Gattegno's work has been in the area of mathematics. His notion of mathematics is based on the theory that in order to generate mental pictures in the learner's mind that are mathematical in character, it is necessary to present situations in which one perceives relationships and their dynamics. Further, the awareness of the dynamics of relationships is equivalent to doing mathematics, and this is fostered by such materials as Cuisenaire rods, Geoboards, and films. Through the use of Gattegno's materials students become actively involved, for they either react directly to objects or perceive directly in organized diagrams that produce the relationships (made evident by the actions or the animation). In effect, students say what they see, thus devolping the language and the notation which translates their awareness. Through this technique it is possible to start from very little and develop a number of units of mathematics independently, breaking the linear sequence of the ordinary curriculum and substituting a multivalent study of pictures. Among the valuable effects of Gattegno's work is the feasibility of beginning mathematics with algebra at the first grade level, and the practicability, through use of equivalences and transformations, of teaching students to compute rapidly and competently. Geometry, as an exciting study of spatial relations, is also introduced at the primary school level thanks to the versatility of geoboards and sets of prisms and cubes; and trigonometry becomes a fascinating game through films that present, literally in minutes, the main trend of the subject. Gattegno is now producing new materials that may change learning situations at the high school level as radically as his previous ones have at the elementary.

With reference to language, the Gattegno materials start on the premise that, since pupils bring to school their spoken speech, writing becomes the learning of a code that transcribes speech, and reading is the decoding of the results. *Words in Color* is the technique worked out to the last detail by Gattegno. Through this technique, Gattegno contends, visual dictation has restored time to its cardinal place in the act of reading; he therefore claims an original solution to a very old problem. Indeed, because of this restoration of time, illiterate adults can pick up reading in hours (rarely more than fifteen), and beginning readers, in about six weeks, reach a level of competence not known so far.

In regard to foreign languages, the *Silent Way* offers a new technique and provides materials which apply to about half a dozen languages. Starting from highly controlled linguistic situations produced with Cuisenaire rods which permit from the start utterance by learners of a number of functional words, the language technique moves through the use of wall charts with colored words printed on them to a fluency of expression that in turn permits the learner in a very short time to behave naturally while using the foreign language. Expansion of the functional language goes on with the rods and charts to a level that makes possible the conquest of luxury vocabularies related to any situation. The materials for this conquest are more conventional than those concerned with the first steps. Gattegno contends that, by using this approach, first year pupils can do the work much better than fourth year students in conventional language teaching.

My personal reaction to Gattegno is one of deepest admiration. I first met him in 1962 when I visited him at his home in Reading, England. Since that time I have carefully studied his materials and observed him in workshops in my own school. In my opinion, this man is indeed a modern Socrates. When Gattegno works with students one can sense, along with the students, his strong feelings for their individual worth as human beings. His influence on education will probably be as great as that of anyone now living.

HOMEWORK—A NEW APPROACH

In the conventional graded school the philosophy of homework has been a kind of dreary "busy work" assignment. More often than not the homework is assigned to keep the student occupied, and frequently it is not even marked and returned after the student hands it in. In the Appropriate Placement school, homework takes the form of private study. It is assigned to: (1) stimulate initiative, response, and self-direction; (2) develop permanent leisure interests in learning; (3) provide practice and application of principles discovered in the learning process. The amount of time spent on private study varies with each student. Factors affecting the time variable are: (1) student age and health; (2) student attitude and interest; (3) student competence in study skills; and (4) student aims and needs.

Private study assignments are planned to meet individual needs. It is simply not possible to do what many graded schools attempt: to list the time to be spent on homework by all students at a given age level. Recognition must be given to the fact that students vary widely in interest from one unit of work to another. Most private study assignments should be long-term assignments in order to give the student practice in budgeting and balancing his time.

The purposes of private home study as far as the student is concerned are: (1) to practice meeting deadlines; (2) to follow a schedule and keep materials in order; (3) to put creative effort in the work; and (4) to hand in on time neat, accurate, and meaningful assignments. From the teacher's standpoint, the purposes are: (1) to encourage learning that is meaningful and useful to the individual; (2) to allow initiative in the student's approach to his assignments; (3) to foster continuing interest in learning; and (4) to help students become increasingly effective in time devoted to individual study.

In order for *any* of these purposes to be realized, *all work completed at home in private study and handed in must be carefully read, corrected, marked, and returned to the student.*

INCREASING INDIVIDUALITY

We are moving, then, from a tightly regimented intermediate school in which students move according to rules, to a school in which students move according to their individual learning performance. In this highly individualized setting the only time students will be put together in groups is when the learning situation can be best promoted by interaction. Self-learning will be a central feature of the curriculum. While this may sound revolutionary at first, it is already happening in the more sensitively taught subjects. Reading and art are examples of this rearrangement. Once the schools seriously commit themselves to the process of individualizing learning, a much wider range in differences in individuals will result. This increase in individuality should alarm no one. *The schools ought to contribute more toward making people different than making people alike.*

If a man does not keep pace with his companions,
perhaps it is because he hears a different drummer.
Let him step to the music which he hears,
however measured or far away.
                                Henry David Thoreau

Chapter Six

THE MULTIPHASED
JUNIOR HIGH SCHOOL

Benjamin Fine, education editor for the North American Newspaper Alliance, focused on the problem of the junior high
school recently in a column which concluded: "We need to
take a good hard look at the junior high school and then abolish
it." At first blush this sounds like violent treatment, but it
expresses the feelings of a good many junior high students and
their parents. The junior high school is suffering from a performance gap between ideals and achievements. The main
trouble lies in the exaggerated emphasis on the physical
changes in students of junior high age. The entire curriculum

has been tied to vague suppositions of the needs of adolescents, rather than clear aims as to the rigor of learning. This philosophy has engulfed the junior high movement and jeopardizes its future, Benjamin Fine is by no means the only commentator on the dreadful outcome of "life adjustment" education. The British scientist C. P. Snow in a recent article for *Look* Magazine warned America:

> Your primary and high school education is much too self-indulgent . . . it is one of the nice things about the American climate of feeling that you passionately desire to make the young happy . . . but . . . you have got to teach your children more if you are going to keep afloat in this stern world.

Most of the general descriptions of the function of the junior high school portray it as an "exploratory" institution. By this is meant that the curriculum should be saturated with courses built around "life adjustment," in which the child can "explore and find himself." This, of course, is educational nonsense. Why should the goal of the junior high school not be that of any other school? Few would question the idea that students must "adapt," but this is not a development lying in the exclusive province of the junior high school. Students of all ages must develop confidence in themselves and in their own destiny. It makes little sense to isolate this feature of the educational process and build the curriculum of the adolescent around it. Actually, the pursuit of knowledge is full of discovery, and the student will have his best exploratory experiences in a vigorous program designed for the cultivation of the mind, rather than one built around "life adjustment" experiences.

It is unfortunate that junior high school teachers have been indoctrinated with the exploratory concepts and the problems of adolescence, with almost complete disregard for subject matter. The training of junior high school teachers has ignored the need for thorough knowledge of a particular discipline. Subject matter is an "extra" for the junior high teacher. This can be seen in the fact that the state of Florida, for example, requires only twelve semester hours of English to qualify as a teacher of that subject in the junior high school. Clearly, twelve semester hours in a discipline is woefully inadequate preparation for teaching anything. In contrast to the minute amount of knowledge required for subject matter, many states require twenty semester hours' training in the vague fields of methodology, growth, and development. Clearly, this is a pitiful attempt at academic standards. The effect of this imprecise training in dubious methodology has been to create a milieu at the junior high school level in which teachers do not know what is expected of them. *They are well prepared to teach something which does not exist.* Furthermore, they fail to realize the satisfactions from teaching, which are enjoyed by teachers in the elementary and senior high schools, simply because they are doing something which they do not understand. And the teacher-training institutions aren't helping; they are continuing to make teachers unfit by casting them in a nonexistent mold.

Administrators of junior high schools who believe that school patrons will continue to tolerate the kind of exploratory nonsense prevalent in the present junior high curriculum are deluding themselves. The mood of the nation towards its schools is undergoing serious changes. There is an ever-increasing demand to replace "life adjustment" programs with good solid basic education, and if this trend continues the junior high school is due for some serious scrutiny.

The Textbook Dilemma

Another major problem of the junior high school is rooted in the fact that, too often the textbook is the course. When the textbook is the dominant material, learning consists only of such things as causes and results of wars, names of various countries, capitals of states, explorers and their activities, spelling words, and trite problems in arithmetic. This means that students are besieged with minutia, and the great themes of the subjects are ignored. Tiny bits of information unrelated to major concepts fail to give students the incentive for curiosity or further inquiry. Textbooks used in the junior high should bear more resemblance to a Kiplinger newsletter with a message that is sharp, clear, and up to date.

Courses in the junior high school must be made *theme-oriented*. The major emphasis should be on the essential principles which hold the subject together. We must change the micro-pedagogy of textbook teaching to a macro-pedagogy in which instructional units are built around underlying principles. The light of curiosity kindled in students' eyes by the excitement of the nongraded years of the early primary grows dim in the fifth and sixth grades and goes out in the seventh and eighth. As one looks into the eyes of junior high students being taught by conventional textbooks, more often than not the reflection he sees is boredom. When the junior high curriculum is examined for innovations, imitation of the high school is seen to be the dominant theme. The only improvements made in the junior high curriculum since its origin are those acquired from the aping of the high school program. This is especially noticeable in the field of foreign languages.

The Importance of Imagination

The junior high school must stop frowning on the goal of development of the imagination. The marvel of imagination is treated by junior high teachers as some monstrous creation to be avoided at any cost. Fantasy, which is what the teachers really fear, is in no way related to imagination; imagining and adventuring should be encouraged. Albert Einstein once advanced the idea that "imagination is more important than knowledge." We need to learn a great deal more about the school climates that foster imagination and creativity, as well as high performance. Imagination deserves to be encouraged as much as does scholarship.

The Nature of Abilities

One of the most important documents ever written on the complex subject of thinking and learning is the *Taxonomy of Educational Objectives* which was edited by Benjamin Bloom. This landmark document's report on the anatomy of abilities has tremendous implications for the junior high school program:

> Although information or knowledge is recognized as an important outcome of education, very few teachers would be satisfied to regard this as the primary or sole outcome of instruction. What is needed is some evidence that the students can do something with their knowledge, that is, that they can apply the information to new situations and problems. It is also expected that students will acquire generalized techniques for dealing with new problems and new materials. Thus, it is expected that when the student encounters a new problem or situation, he will select an appropriate technique for attacking it and will bring to bear the necessary information, both facts and principles. This has been labeled "critical thinking" by some, "reflective thinking" by Dewey and others, and "problem solving" by still others. In the taxonomy we have used the term "intellectual abilities and skills." The most general operational definition of these abilities and skills is that the individual can find appropriate information and techniques in his previous experience to bring to bear on new problems and situations. This requires some analysis or understanding of the new situation; it requires a background of knowledge or methods which can be readily utilized; and it also requires some facility in discerning the appropriate relations between previous experience and the new situation.[1]

---

[1] *Taxonomy of Educational Objectives,* Benjamin S. Bloom, Editor. David McKay Company, Inc., New York, 1956, p. 38.

The Ultimate Curriculum

What will the curriculum be like when it is finally developed? The program of studies will be organized around the major concepts of each discipline, and subject matter will be related to these themes. The principles of each subject will be so clear that they will simply fall out of the instruction. In this arrangement, it will be easy to construct a curriculum phased so that it can be coupled to the intellectual development of individuals. The structure of subjects will be further strengthened by an approach to learning which embodies the techniques of discovery and quest as the major tools of the learner. For example, the learner will be taught to look at art through the eyes of the artist and at science with the perception of the scientist. The study of history will become an examination of historical documents which the student views through the eyes of the historian.

Admittedly this program will be a long time in coming. What should the innovative-minded school principal and searcher do while waiting for these developments? Much can be accomplished if the school will carefully scrutinize the materials it uses as well as the calibre of its instructional staff. Appropriate materials should be constructed largely around problem-solving techniques. Teachers should develop individual artistry designed to make students more curious and inquiring. Critical thinking should be vigorously encouraged. The junior high school should realize that the nation's scholars are now writing new course material built around the central themes of subjects. It is time for junior high teachers to stop preparing curriculum guides, and begin to spend more time re-designing the structure of the school to accommodate differences in learning rates. A curriculum probe directed toward the individual is more urgently needed at the junior high level than at any other, because the junior high enrolls students ranging more widely in height, weight, knowledge and maturity than any other kind of school.

New Purposes

The most important objective is this: *education at the junior high school level should shift from the school to the individual the responsibility for pursuing his own education.* While this may seem at first to be unrealistic, one should bear in mind that children learn best, not when they are taught, but when they learn for themselves.

New Components in the Curriculum

The nongraded school has sparked a variety of curriculum innovations. One of the most interesting is the idea that subject matter disciplines should be presented in three multistages:

1. *The factual stage* which is concerned with mastery of the fundamental aspects of the course. This is usually accomplished through formal class sessions. The object is to give a common foundation upon which the individual can build.
2. *The discovery stage* which is accomplished through closely directed projects based on the factual phase. The class should be organized around the seminar approach and each student must have an opportunity to present his own seminar.
3. *The inquiry stage* which is concerned with research in considerable depth. Here the inquiring mind can pursue learning far beyond the limits of the ordinary classroom.

It is time for the junior high to be organized on a different basis from that of the graded organization and its graded textbooks. The new junior high organization must be nongraded in order that it can accommodate a wide spread of achievement. One of the best analyses ever made of the extent of variability among students was contained in a report made several years ago by Walter Cook, Dean of the College of Education of the University of Minnesota. The gist of this report supports strongly the kind of curriculum being urged for the junior high school:

The Extent of Variability

When a random group of six-year-olds enters the first grade, two percent of them will be below the average four-year-old in general mental development, and two percent will be above the average eight-year-old. Disregarding the extreme two percent at either end, there is a four year range in general intelligence. By the time this group has reached the age of twelve (seventh grade level), the range will have increased to almost eight years. As long as all the children of all the people remain in school, the range continues to increase. When the educational achievement of a typical sixth grade class is measured, we find a range of approximately eight years in reading comprehension, vocabulary, arithmetic reasoning, arithmetic computation, mechanics of English composition, and other forms of achievement. In almost any sixth grade class will be found a pupil with first or second grade reading ability, and another with eleventh or twelfth grade reading ability. In any grade above the primary level will be found the complete range of elementary school achievement.

At the high-school and college levels, Learned and Wood have given us an answer. When the *General Culture Battery,* consisting of achievement tests in general science, foreign literature, fine arts and social studies, was administered to high school and college seniors in Pennsylvania, it was found that the upper ten percent of high school seniors were above the college senior median and could have been given B.A. degrees without lowering the intellectual standards of such degrees. It was also found that the lower ten percent of college seniors were below the high school senior median.

The Public Should Learn the Facts

Although these facts should be basic data in educational thinking and call for a revision of our postulates, they are largely ignored. The idea that the process of schooling *must* consist of homogeneous groups of pupils receiving uniform instruction by mass educational techniques from uniform textbooks is the axiom which prevents constructive approaches to the problem of variability in the classroom. It leads to the further assumptions that grade levels should signify rather definite states of educational achievement; that the course of study for a grade is the prescribed academic requirement, to be administered uniformly to all pupils; that the pupil should not be promoted to a grade until he is able to do the work outlined for that grade; that when individual differences are provided for by good teaching, all pupils can be brought up to standard; that maintaining a passing mark results in homogeneous instructional groups; and that when relative homogeneity does not prevail, it is a result of poor teaching or lax standards. These assumptions are contrary to fact. *It is time the public* learned the facts. The range of ability in the classes of the elementary and high school is so great that if the slow learner in the eighth grade were demoted to the fourth, he would still be a slow learner in the fourth, and below the median of the class. If the top pupil of the fourth grade were accelerated to the eighth, he would still be a bright pupil in the eighth, and above the median of that class.[2]

The Changing Role of Instruction

An intent of the multiphased curriculum is to force the teacher to be more intellectually honest than he has been in the past. He must be as aware of his own intellectual potential as he is that of his students. The teacher must be willing to state frankly: "I don't know all of the answers but let's talk about it." The idea is to strip the curriculum of authoritarianism. The teacher doesn't know the answers, and the research scientist doesn't know the answers. This type of learning situation stimulates some intriguing and shrewd guesses on the part of the student. The process of learning moves naturally into the realm of intuitive thinking.

---

[2] *The Gifted and the Retarded in Historical Perspective,* Walter W. Cook, Phi Delta Kappan, March, 1958.

Principles of Multiphasing

The application of the principles of multiphasing at the junior high school level requires that students be grouped on the basis of either aptitude or achievement or both. All students should be carefully tested, and recently developed tests should be used, since some of the older ones are too fact-centered to be useful. Students who score in the lower percentiles of achievement in a given subject must be tested further with aptitude and nonverbal tests. The purpose is to ascertain their particular needs and provide the kind of curriculum needed by each individual. Once the requirements of the entire student body are known, the school can then plan its phased curriculum.

The number of phases in the new junior high school will depend on two factors: the number of students enrolled and the cultural and socio-economic background of the student body. A large junior high school will normally contain five phases ranging from honors work for the quick to remedial for the slow. A small school, which may need five phases because of a wide spread of achievement, may have to limit its differentiation to three because of its limited population.

MULTIPHASED GROUPING

A typical organization for an average junior high school enrolling 1000 students.

Student's Percentile of Achievement *Phase*	0 to 20 Phase 1	20 to 40 Phase 2	40 to 60 Phase 3	60 to 80 Phase 4	80 to 100 Phase 5
		Numbers of Students			
English	100	200	400	200	100
Mathematics	75	225	400	225	75
Science	60	200	440	200	60
Social Science	105	100	460	150	135

The number of students in a particular phase will vary from community to community, as this factor is based to a considerable extent on the cultural development of the individuals who comprise the population of the school.

MULTIPHASED GROUPING

A typical organization for an average junior high school enrolling 200 students.

Student's Percentile of Achievement	0 to 30	30 to 70	70 to 90
Phase	Phase 1	Phase 2	Phase 3
Numbers of Students			
English	25	150	25
Mathematics	50	100	50
Science	30	80	90
Social Science	40	120	40

Principles of Phasing

1. Students should be grouped on the basis of either aptitude or achievement, or both.
2. Before placing a student in a subject, the school must determine the phase at which he can most profitably enter it.
3. A student's entry into the phase of a subject as well as his exit from it must be determined by proven evidence of his knowledge of the subject.
4. Under the phased curriculum the student is always working at the proper point since his curriculum is geared to his own maximum achievement.
5. The phased curriculum must be designed in such a fashion that it will have special appeal at the student's first exit point from the school, which is usually sixteen.
6. The material of courses must not only be phased but spiraled. The phase is the vehicle for upward movement.

The curriculum spiral is different from the conventional spiral of a spring which merely spirals upward. In the spiral curriculum, at every turn there is a change in diameters. In essence, since the spiral curriculum is based on the idea of reinforcement, then each spiral forward has a broader academic base than the diameter of the previous spiral.

Ideally a multiphased curriculum for the junior high will have a "built in" experimental factor. The moment that a new practice appears to be successful, plans should be formulated for making it obsolete. It is much too easy for a promising new experiment to become a dull old orthodoxy. If an innovation is really successful, it should engender further innovations. Perhaps this could be more easily accomplished if every school had a vice-principal in charge of heresy.

Unfortunately, the major changes in schools have been concerned with the addition of factors which don't really make any difference. A classic example of this is the current "enrichment" vogue, based on the theory that you can add a new concept while continuing the old one. This is not what is needed, since the schools eventually go back to the old practice where they feel more comfortable. What schools should do is change the entire practice.

The New Role of the Counselor

Individualized progress will require a great deal more academic counseling than has been available in the past. This calls for a different and more substantial training of counselors. The present training of guidance counselors is largely in the area of educational psychology, and the finished product is something of a pseudo-psychologist. The result is that much of the nation's student talent is being wasted because of poor and indifferent counseling. The student's success in the present setting is determined by how well he fits into the existing curriculum, whereas it should be a matter of how well the curriculum adapts to his requirements. In the future, the emphasis on counselor training will center around academic counseling and individual learning rather than the fuzzy theories of educational psychology. To prepare him for this role, the counselor's training must be heavily concentrated in the four basic academic areas of the curriculum. He will need a better background in English, mathematics, history and science, and much of his educational psychology training should be discarded.

They do not serve who only stand and wait.

John F. Morse

Chapter Seven

THE MULTIPHASED

SENIOR HIGH SCHOOL

Typical of comments about nongraded Appropriate Placement
high schools are the following:

> The most immediate and startling impression I had of the
> school generally, an impression that deepened as the day wore
> on, is that this school is run for the sake of the students—not to
> entertain them or to keep them off the streets or to baby-sit
> them, but to change them intellectually. It is run less for the
> convenience of the administrators and teachers and janitors
> than any school I've ever seen.

> Since the whole school staff is more fully focused on the
> observation and assessment of individual student learning than

any high school staff I have ever known, my first and strongest inclination is to spy on the school activity to discover how they got to be that way.[1]

The unusual and complex course titles accurately reflect the spirit of what is probably the most unusual, complex, and exciting public school in America—Melbourne High.[2]

The great majority of Melbourne students, of course, are . . . as at any other school . . . neither geniuses or dullards. But at Melbourne there is prevailing excitement that somehow catches up with nearly everybody.[3]

Because of these and myriad other similar statements by qualified educators and veteran newsmen, it indeed appears that something unusual is occurring in Appropriate Placement schools.

The conventional approach to secondary education indicates that knowledge is neatly arranged, organized, and stable. But, on the contrary, knowledge is unique, unarranged, and unpredictable. Often it is best absorbed when assaulted in unconventional fashion. The multiphased approach to learning is a vehicle providing a radically different kind of learning situation—one which challenges not only the quick and the slow but also the creative. Meaningful learning is concerned not merely with hard work but the creative process as well.

The multiphased curriculum frees schools from the usual artificial pressures of social peer groups which foster conformity by afflicting and tyrannizing adolescent life. Students are taught as individuals rather than prisoners of the group. Prerogatives such as senior privileges have no place in secondary schools which have deep commitments to learning. High schools organized around the phase concept are mo-

---

[1] John Dobbin, Educational Testing Service, memo to the ETS staff concerning his visit to Melbourne High School, March 22, 1963.

[2] "Revolt in Education," *Newsweek*, 60, 15:109–112, October 8, 1962.

[3] Lapham, L., "High School Where the Sky's the Limit," The Saturday Evening Post, 235, 45:75–79, December 15, 1962.

tivated to strive continuously toward the goal of involving more and more students in the process of independent study and individual learning. The ultimate destination is an exotic learning situation in which many high school students will receive their education by appointment. The accent of the multiphased process is on accessibility, making the creative components of the school available after school and in the evenings. Easy access to labs and libraries creates a setting which fosters independent study. The multiphased senior high school can offer the kind of educational program which has in the past been provided only by the better liberal arts colleges, but teachers must rise to the occasion. They must realize that motivation is the master key to learning, and that the faculty of a school can create an atmosphere in which learning is serious, personal and absorbing. The impact of multiphasing on the curriculum and its influence on each subject is discussed one subject at the time.

English

Just as the most important subject in the elementary school is reading, the most significant high school subject is its sophisticated counterpart, English. It is indeed unfortunate to have to report that the most important subject in the high school is in a muddled state of intellectual disrepair. U.S. Commissioner of Education Francis Keppel recently described English teaching as "in critical need of increased, active, and vigorous support." James R. Squire, the executive secretary of the National Council of English teachers goes much farther when he warns that "without reforms, English classes across the country will go on wallowing in dull, lifeless teaching, devoid of one iota of excitement." With everybody rushing around to save English from itself the true picture of English is obscured. The College Entrance Examination Board has set up a Commission on English, the U.S. Office of Education has diverted federal funds to what is called "Project English," and the National Council of Teachers of English have their own pet solutions under way. Most of these schemes have been buttressed with the largesse of foundation funds. Now, what is the true status of English as a school subject? The individual who should know best is Floyd Rinker, Executive Director of the Commission of English of the College Entrance Examination Board. In a recent item in *Time Magazine*, Mr. Rinker is quoted as describing the status of English with these mournful words: "Every morning I awake with an empty feeling as if there had been a death in the family."

Why is Mr. Rinker so disconsolate? And how did English get into such a state?

The Grammar Problem

1. Grammar is universally poorly taught by teachers who don't know the subject. Most English teachers haven't had a course in English grammar since leaving high school, and are still teaching the same inaccurate grammar in the same old unimaginative way that it was taught to them.
2. Grammar is unpleasant and poorly taught—yet, it is monotonously reviewed every year.
3. The grammatical lore preached in the schools today is illogical, incorrect, and inaccurate.
4. We have taught English in the dichotomy of "right or wrong."
5. We bewilder students by the way we teach. It is a manifest impossibility for a child to speak the way he writes, yet we would have him do so. A key point of the linguist is that a language is primarily a spoken language. The written form is derivative.

I think I can illustrate the distressing state of affairs with an experience which I had in the sixth grade. I discovered early in the year that my English teacher could diagram only certain kinds of sentences, and thereafter I spent a great deal of time making up sentences I knew she could not diagram. Her somewhat violent reaction was to take me aside one day and threaten me with a vigorous whipping. This little lady is probably still in an elementary school somewhere teaching the same old incompetent brand of grammar. It used to be that if a teacher wanted to get into trouble with the P. T. A. all she had to do was let the word get around that she wasn't teaching grammar any more. In the age of the hydrogen bomb, the American people have suddenly become ambivalent, and we should take advantage of this vacillation to rid ourselves of the antiquated shibboleth of normative grammar.

Reading

We can't talk about the plight of English without saying something about the dreadful state of reading. Reading is the most important subject in the curriculum, yet the experts cannot agree on how it should be taught. On one side we have the phonics group insisting upon phonetic analysis as the superior method. At the opposite pole we find the sight-reading crowd advocating what they call the "look-say" method. In between these two points of view we find primary teachers floundering between loyalty to one method or the other or a combination of both. The seriousness of the problem is neatly illustrated by an incident which happened last year when the Ford Foundation set up a conference between leading advocates of the sight-reading method and leaders of the phonics technique. The objective was to determine the components of a good reading program. The differences between the two points of view proved so bitter that the conference erupted in violent disagreement, and when the embers had cooled, conference minutes revealed two conclusions: 1. "Reading is a problem"; 2. "My way is best." No wonder "Johnny can't read." Senior high schools are literally overrun with students who cannot read above the fourth grade level. As a result, high school English is unable to move freely in its proper sphere. English is now largely a subject without shape or form as an effective instrument of education. The past attitude toward change in the teaching of English might well be described by a remark once made by the great French statesman Talleyrand: "And above all, not too much zeal!"

English teachers and schools can no longer solve their problems intramurally. Change is so rapid on the education scene that we now have to look to projects like the Commission on English and the U.S. Office of Education's "Project English" for leadership. But, about all that they have done to date is succeed in fogging the issue more. Mr. Rinker's great sorrow has, as yet, failed to produce any solution.

The currently popular view of English is that it should be taught as a tripod consisting of proportionate parts of composition, literature, and language. Whatever theoretical support this tripod may have, it will surely collapse unless a new leg is added: the most important subject in the school curriculum is reading and it is high time that reading came to high school. Every elementary, junior high, and senior high school should teach three kinds of reading:

1. A continuing remedial program for students who cannot learn easily.
2. A developmental program for students who need it.
3. A speed-reading program involving sophisticated techniques such as skimming and rapid comprehension. (Skimming is nothing more than a prelude to reading, searching the pages of a book for an individual item or for a general approach to the organizational pattern of an article.)

Keeping Abreast of Change

In an era of cybernation in which the linguists have set themselves up as a rescue squad to save English from itself, English teachers must dispel images which they acquired 25 or 30 years ago. Keats once said, "English must be kept up." The problem is now more acute and the plight of the English teacher is better described by a passage from *Alice in Wonderland* to the effect that, "you have to keep running just to keep up."

The first step to nongrading an English program is to cut out the mass of detail which makes the English classroom a spiritless climate for learning. The next action is to take off the academic bridle which restrains youngsters intellectually. Consider as an example the ninth grade student who scores grade 13 on an achievement test. It is absurd to make this youngster go through English 10, English 11, and English 12. In a multiphased curriculum, he is placed in an open-ended college-level Advanced Placement English where he remains for three years. By the same token, it is a conspiracy of nonsense to give 10th grade students who read at the third grade level a state-adopted 10th grade textbook and expect that they will read *Macbeth*. We have tried too long to ram Shakespeare down throats too narrow for *Rebecca of Sunnybrook Farm*. In the multiphased English program, the below-standard student is assigned *two* periods of English daily. These double-period English classes are geared to the student's level of achievement. Reading and writing should be the basic program in any school and every other subject can be suspended until a student learns to read and write with competence.

The organization of the multiphased English curriculum is as follows:

Phase 1—A curriculum designed for students who are deficient in reading.

Phase 2—A vigorous program of basic communication skills for marginal students.

Phase 3—Beyond basic education for the student who learns in an average way.

Phase 4—A curriculum with depth and concentration in the elements of composition and literature.

Phase 5—Advanced Placement English for students who are able to earn college credit while still in high school.

This realignment of students brings about a major difference in course content from that of the conventionally graded school. The motion of the nongraded curriculum compels the school to resort to a much wider range of materials and a more vigorous program. None of the mediocre standard textbooks are usable in any phase, and a multiplicity of material must replace them. A multiphased curriculum designed for student mobility must be saturated with variegated materials. When these changes are wrought the advanced contours of the curriculum begin to look like a Rorschach Test. The result is an unceasing problem-solving atmosphere.

The effect of multiphasing English is to change the subject matter on a continuing rather than a yearly basis. Learning is both more appropriate and more stimulating when students of comparable linguistic skills and academic accomplishment are grouped together. In a multiphased English program considerable attention must be paid to the matter of a flexible design which will accommodate the concept that students should be mobile—able to advance from one phase of learning to a higher phase at any time. An easy way of providing basic material planned for mobile situations is to upset the conventional arrangement in which 10th grade students study American literature, 11th grade students study English literature and 12th grade students study World literature. A natural situation accommodating mobility is created when *all* students study American literature at one time, *all* English, and *all* World. Then, when a student is accelerated from one phase to a higher phase he continues with the same material but in greater depth. Let me assure you that if the I.B.M. machines which group youngsters in conventional schools made a mistake and they were scheduled into English 4 before English 3, it wouldn't make a great deal of difference in academia.

Another reform which is spurred by nongraded education is a change in the function of the teacher. Students who are unbridled intellectually are no longer content with a passive kind of education which is mostly telling. Teachers must throw out "the old kit bag." I think I can best describe the kind of teacher I am talking about here with an incident I observed in a class recently. The teacher was giving a test in English and the first question written on the chalkboard was: "Which of the required reading did you find least interesting?" After members of the class had had ten minutes to expatiate on what was to them a very congenial topic, the teacher wrote the second question which asked: "To what defect in yourself do you attribute this lack of interest?"

THE MULTIPHASED ENGLISH CURRICULUM

Now, what kind of materials should an imaginative and venturesome teacher use? In phases 3, 4, and 5 the courses should be built around paperbacks, and the teacher should use lots of them. The textbook must be thrown away. In its place, there should be innumerable paperbacks containing essays, short stories, plays, novels and poetry collections. Each teacher should have the freedom to design his own speaking, writing, and listening activities around a group of selected paperback titles. There are many advantages to having students buy their own paperbacks. First, this allows the individual student to underscore the ideas which appeal to him. Secondly, it gets him in the habit of owning books.

In the place of grammar the teacher should teach the mechanics and technology of the language. English technology should be taught in the context of the literary discussions and compositions which arise from classroom activity. The teacher should abandon the ancient practice of teaching grammar in an isolated situation. In the way of curriculum priorities, reading comes first in the long list of essentials in the curriculum. It must be recognized that reading is basic for learning in all subjects and students must learn to read with precision and comprehension.

Phase 1

Phase 1 laboratories in reading and writing offer a sanctuary for learning to those high school students who are so disadvantaged that they are virtually non-readers and unable to write either a legible or meaningful sentence. These are the students who test under a fifth-grade reading level, a group roughly in the lower tenth percentile in verbal achievement. Since the Phase 1 student is sorely behind in the verbal skills needed to learn fundamentals, he is required to enroll in two periods of English a day: a laboratory for writing and another for reading. Each laboratory is limited to an enrollment of under fifteen students at a time. In this setting the teacher can more efficiently adapt methods and materials to each student, and more easily maintain the friendly relationships necessary if such students are to learn.

In many respects the curriculum in Phase 1 English is the verbal arts curriculum of the first five grades; but since the students range in age from fifteen to twenty-one, it is important that the approach be sophisticated. Much attention is given to providing reading material that has an elementary vocabulary but an adolescent or adult interest-level. Teaching is aimed always toward providing these students with skills and a psychological climate that will achieve their wanting to read, their gaining the courage, confidence and ability to try material of ever-increasing difficulty.

Phase 2

In the Phase 2 reading laboratory the student who learns modestly is given instruction and drill in line with his individual needs. Reading skills are developed by continuing the development of those already begun in Phase 1, plus an introduction to more complicated skills. Among new skills introduced are reading for inference, comparison and analogy, together with more extensive use of the dictionary. Concentration is also focused on vocabulary-building. Exposure to vocabulary is increased to approximately the eighth-grade level. The method is through a phonetic, structural, graphematic, and contextual attack on words. Students are encouraged to read according to their interests and abilities and to read for content of ideas communicated as well as to read ambitiously. Ample opportunity and materials are provided for free reading at school, and all materials are presented in an attractive manner.

In the Phase 2 writing laboratory, writing is stressed as a vital force in the adequate use of the language. The student is encouraged to develop pride in handwriting, and to maintain high standards of legibility, as well as to write with accuracy and some speed. The student is taught spelling, sentence structure, recognition and use of the topic sentence, adequate organization of material, and all necessary mechanics needed to help him interpret and express the meaning of his varied experiences.

Phase 3

Phase 3 English students in the Appropriate Placement school (those of average ability) study five genres—the novel, the short story, the essay, the drama, and poetry. Each teacher chooses selections for consideration with regard to literary merit and technique, and student interest and understanding. Mechanical "tools" (i.e. spelling, punctuation, vocabulary, usage, sentence structure) are taught functionally as students learn to write under a policy of steady composition, carefully directed and corrected by both student and teacher. Themes are largely expository and subject matter is related to the literature.

Phase 4

The expectation level in Phase 4 English is high. The students engaged in this program have already proved themselves in English achievement tests. Phase 4 students come into the program highly motivated and ready for challenge from their fellows, their teachers, and from the content of the course itself. These students stimulate one another in their ability to work with their peers in small groups; they possess the maturity to accept the sometimes lonely and often rewarding role of individual pursuit in English. Formal grammar is not taught, *per se*, yet any student weak in grammar is expected to seek the needed help and rectify the problem. Rather, the emphasis is on continual practice in all kinds of writing, with examination of writing samples; and on the study and analysis of provocative, difficult selections in literature. An understanding of the various literary forms is required, and always quality and depth of study are valued over hurried surveys of masses of material. Themes and concepts are important, and basic logic and semantics are introduced. Clear, thoughtful, and effective oral and written communication is the daily objective.

Phase 5

Phase 5 English is based on the advanced placement program of the College Entrance Examination Board. The intent of this course is to prepare the student who wishes to seek advanced standing when he enters college. This phase offers students of talent and achievement in English a course structured to develop thinking in depth in literature, and how to write critically on the ensuing discoveries. The class works together in analysis, but it is the student's scholarship in private study that aids him in developing independence in the learning process.

THE NEW SCIENCE CURRICULA

The New Physics

In the remaking of American education few men have played a more important role than Jerrold Zacharias. A distinguished nuclear physicist, member of the President's Science Advisory Committee and director of M.I.T.'s famous Radiation Laboratory, Dr. Zacharias in 1956 addressed himself to the task of improving the subject matter of high school physics. Under his direction a committee of national scholars developed a whole new approach to the teaching of science. In the process they completely revolutionized the high school physics course. Zacharias estimates that the new physics eliminates at least fifty percent of the old course. For purposes of administration the physics reform group called themselves the Physical Science Study Committee, hence the name P.S.S.C. Physics.

The new physics course abandoned the old notion of presenting physics on the basis of authority. The improved course is designed in such fashion that it leads students to think like physicists. The student is encouraged to test every single hypothesis and to accept nothing as fact until it has been clearly demonstrated in the laboratory. The reform of physics not only created an exciting new course in physics; it had the effect of setting in motion the machinery for scientists in other disciplines to improve their subjects in like fashion.

B. S. C. S. Biology

Sparked by the brilliant achievements of the new physics study, the American Institute of Biological Sciences, in 1959, established the Biological Sciences Curriculum Study for the purpose of improving the subject matter and teaching of high school biology. The new materials developed by the Biological Sciences Curriculum Study have been constructed to emphasize investigation and inquiry as the means of acquiring significant knowledge in science.

Since 1962 B. S. C. S. materials have been generally available to secondary schools who wish to use the new material in their biology courses. Perhaps even more important than the curriculum reform of the general biology course is a project more recently undertaken by the group. In the fall of 1963 about a dozen selected schools were invited to experiment with new materials which had been developed specifically for the slow learner. The significance of this development is that this is the first time that a group of national scholars has endeavored to construct course material specifically for the below-average student. This is a crucially important event since thirty percent of high school students have been dropping through the planks of the educational structure, largely because of an inappropriate curriculum. In the summer of 1964 the B. S. C. S. materials for the slow learner were further revised and are now more broadly available. Their influence will be great.

THE HUMANITIES

The school year 1963 witnessed a burgeoning interest in high school courses in the humanities. The general pattern seems to be a course taught by a team of teachers, most often consisting of a music teacher, an art teacher, and a history teacher. On the other hand, numbers of schools have developed one-teacher humanities courses which have been carried out quite successfully. While the introduction of humanities courses into the high school is relatively new, there is no question about the need of providing instruction in this important area to all students; consequently, each school should phase this subject along the lines set forth in the section on English.

No one is in a better position to describe the rapid growth of humanities courses at the high school level than Charlie Keller, director of a foundation whose sole purpose is to advance the influence of the humanities. Speaking recently on the status of humanities courses in the high school, Keller reported: [4]

"I have become convinced that just about the most interesting and important development in American education these days is the appearance of interdisciplinary humanities courses in schools here and there throughout the country, taught sometimes by teams of history, English, music, and art teachers. And these courses are not just for students who are going on to college. Indeed, I am just as interested in such courses for students whose formal education will end with graduation from high school or even the tenth grade.

A definition is in order. In terms of what they're not, the humanities are those areas of learning which are not included in the sciences and the social sciences; but to be more positive, the humanities embrace literature, languages, history, music, art, and philosophy. Originally the humanities meant only the classics; the scope of subjects has been greatly widened. In broader terms, the humanities acquaint man with the thoughts, creations, and activities of his predecessors through the ages, and of mankind around him. They tell him about his roots, his origins, and his neighbors. They impel him to ask the grave and constant questions, and to ponder answers.

---

[4] Talk given by Charles Keller at the Fall Meeting of the New England Association of Teachers of English, Manchester, Vermont. September 1963.

I urge the humanistic approach in all teaching, in all living. This approach views man in his proper relationship to the things about him. It provides men with needed strength outside themselves, and gives them confidence that men make history, that men can "ride things" and not things men. Ralph Waldo Emerson expressed the essence of the humanities when he wrote:

> Every revolution was once a thought in one man's mind, and when the same thought occurs to another man, it is the key to an era. Every reform was first a private opinion, and when it shall be a private opinion once again, it will solve the problems of the age.

The humanistic approach leads men to think about values. It establishes that within certain limits men have choices among alternatives, that these choices represent a treasured part of freedom and should be made carefully and thoughtfully, that making a choice is an act, and that acts have consequences. The humanistic approach, plus a deep knowledge of the humanities, can enable men to live excitingly and effectively both with themselves and in a world which badly needs men and women with courage based on knowledge.

Knowing what men have thought, said, written, created, and done in the past enables one to see more clearly the present and the future. In the humanities is found, not escape into the past, but strength for the present and the future. Clifton Fadiman has written that the source of our present trouble lies "in the circumstances that somehow people do not know who they are, where they are, or how they got there. If nothing in their . . . education has convinced them that Newton, Shakespeare, and Lincoln are both more interesting and more admirable than Frank Sinatra, Jerry Lewis and Pat Boone, they will find answers to their questions in Sinatra, Lewis and Boone and not in Newton, Shakespeare and Lincoln.

A student should identify himself with the past in the way which Emerson highlighted when he wrote:

> There is a relation between the hours of our life and the centuries of time. . . . I have no expectation that any man will read history aright who thinks that what was done in a remote age, by men whose names have resounded far, has any deeper sense than what he is doing today.

From a study of the humanities will come a knowledge of the values which have stood the test of time and which give men convictions and the courage to stand by for them. Further, it will engender a desire to search for truth, an awareness of the excitement of life which can lessen the boredom that is too much with us, and a perception of human roots that give stability. Study of the humanities will help us as we strive for international peace; it serves such worthy ends as respect for the individual, intellectual humility, and emotional stability."

In conclusion, any blueprint for Space Age Education must place a great deal of stress upon learning in the humanities for all students. While this subject in the past has been taught exclusively to the talented and gifted students, increased leisure time due to the effects of automation and cybernation make it important for every individual to have an understanding and appreciation of this important subject.

Art

The teaching of art in the schools will at last come into its own—and here I am not talking about the clay-thumping and wire-bending activities which make up the conventional school art program. I refer to thorough courses in the appreciation and understanding of art. Other learning in this field will comprise thorough training in the principles of drawing, painting and sculpture, with courses in depth for the more talented. Only some five percent of the students in the nation's high schools are pursuing courses in art. In the era of a Great Society, from seventy-five to a hundred percent of the students in high school should study art in some form. The excitement of a real art course in all its dimensions is described by a sculpture student at Melbourne High School: [5]

> The wire was difficult to work with and the results were unpredictable. The shape you treasured on Monday you squashed on Tuesday. When the movement was right the balance was wrong. If, perchance, you happened to stumble across an acceptable piece your next problem was greater.
>
> The plaster was runny and drippy, hard and crumbly. The texture impossible to control. The wire lost all shape and the plaster filled the wrong holes. Still it held some resemblance to the first shape. After the first day with the plaster the second was a delight and the shape became "something." Ideas form as well as bumps and when the plastering is dry and the sanding is started the real feeling begins. If the relationship is right you will have to touch the piece to get the real meaning.
>
> To say what I learned in certain words is impossible. My hands learned more than I can say.

Mathematics

There is no greater evidence of change in the academic world than that happening in mathematics. For centuries mathematics was thought to be unchangeable and it was taught in a rigid and inflexible framework. By contrast, mathematical education in the Spage Age must be under constant scrutiny and must constantly undergo change. The development of a technologically oriented society makes it increasingly necessary that mathematical education be kept up to date. It must fill the needs of an advancing and advanced community.

In the phased curriculum the needs of students can be easily accommodated. Some high school students spend all of their time in mathematics working on manipulative skills while

---

[5] Mardie Lyman, Sculpture Class, October 1964.

others are ready to probe deeply in the areas of problem-solving through work in probability, linear algebra and calculus. The mathematics program for both the slow and the fast students should be organized around the "directed discovery" approach. The notion of letting the student discover for himself must pervade the entire program. Sometimes the discovery approach will be precipitated casually, other times it will be vigorously stimulated by the teacher.

History

In the multiphased process, history courses are organized into research and discussion classes. They are set up along flexible lines so that students spend a considerable part of each class week in the library. The new approach is described by Priscilla Griffith, history teacher at Melbourne High School, in the course description of the class in International Affairs:

"The first nine weeks, or longer (whatever develops as the most useful unit of time) is devoted to the study of five "models" projected by Dr. Saul Mendlevitz. These are the versions of what the world will be like within the next fifty years. They are:

1. The Protracted Conflict Model in which the next fifty years will be occupied by a sustained conflict between the USSR and the USA for world domination.
2. The Bi-Polar Model in which the world will already be divided between the above-mentioned powers.
3. Regionalism Model in which development will be along the lines of regional groupings such as the European Commonmarket.
4. Polyeentrism Model in which the development will be just the same as now with a mixture of over 100 sovereign nations conducting special separate foreign policies utilizing the U.N. to varying degrees (the U.N. representing the approach of collective security).

5. The Clark-Sehn Revisions of the U.N. Charter which more or less move toward more international law; not, however, world government.

We study how conflicts between nations may be settled in each of these systems, looking for the best peace system. During the remainder of the school year, we do individual research on problems such as the French-Algerian Conflict, the Panama Canal Problem, the Isreali-Suez Crisis, the Cuban Missile Crisis, etc. These problems are handled as case studies so that the students (each on a project of his own choosing) can use the problem in each of the five models and come to some conclusions about peace systems on the basis of his own research. A major objective of this course is for each individual to build his own working bibliography in this field."

The new emphasis in the teaching of history should center around studies and discussions of the great documents and significant movements rather than the great men in history.

Home Economics

More and more frequently the question arises: what changes are being made in such courses as Home Economics? Mrs. J. Newman, chairman of the home economics department at Melbourne High School, describes the changes as follows:

"One of the objectives of concept-centered education is for the students to learn the principles of a subject and how to manipulate them in varying and often new combinations.

"Home Economics is a discipline unto itself but it also borrows from other educational disciplines and gives the student practice in applying principles in these combinations as no other subject can. The principle of design and color, for example, are applied in table-setting, flower-arranging, house-planning, landscaping, clothing, and on into an endless list of related subjects. Nowhere else is the fact that we are part of a constantly changing world easier to stress and re-emphasize than with the subject matter of instant mashed potatoes and miracle fabrics or dresses made of paper that you can wear and throw away, perhaps.

"The type of educational training that does not result in a student learning 'what kind of a job he is out of' is particularly evident in those with home economics backgrounds. They are welcomed for jobs ranging in variety from elementary education teachers to preparing the foods for the astronauts on their trip to the moon, or managing a furniture store. This seems to be concrete evidence that the frequent practical application of broad principles does result in adaptability."

The New Concept of Large Group Instruction

The term "large group instruction" has become associated almost entirely with the concept of team teaching. This is an extremely unfortunate development since the most successful large group instruction is accomplished in single teaching rather than in team situations. It has recently become clear that certain high school subjects can be taught effectively to very large groups—sixty or more students—by just one teacher. This figure is used since normal class size is generally understood to mean thirty students. The dividend which derives from large group instruction with one teacher in charge is the opportunity for redeployment of staff. For example, when a typing class is increased from the conventional 30 to 100 students, two teachers are relieved for redeployment to other classes. Surplus staff should be redeployed among the academic subjects where teachers are traditionally overworked.

Typewriting

Typing is a prime example of a skill subject well suited to large group instruction. To teach typing in anything but a large group is both inefficient and uneconomical. Since the process by which one learns to type consists entirely of mastering a finger dexterity skill, adroiteness in this craft must be self-learned. The process is composed of about ninety-five percent practice with no more than five percent instruction.

In large schools the minimum size of typing classes should be 100 students. There is no maximum. Since instructional presentation is minimal in this subject, five classes consisting of a hundred and fifty students to the class is not an excessive load for a typing teacher. Whenever the structure of a subject requires abbreviated instruction, the class should be reorganized so that one teacher can direct a large number of students.

The matter of providing space for such a large group may present a problem since conventional schools contain classrooms which were constructed to house a maximum of 35 to 40 students per class. This handicap can be overcome in one of two ways. Where the walls are not loadbearing, the sledge hammer technique will eliminate partitions and increase class size. In locations where the adjacent walls are load-bearing, the problem can be solved by wiring two or more nearby rooms to the same intercom system. The visible presence of the teacher every moment is unnecessary in typing classes. Well-executed instructions and occasional monitoring will suffice.

Shorthand

Another subject which may be efficiently taught to large groups by one teacher is shorthand. The learning of shorthand comprises a mixture of listening, writing and typing. This knack is best learned in an electro-mechanical laboratory equipped with tape recorders and earphones. Through these devices each student is able to listen, take dictation, and transcribe at his own rate. The recommended minimum class size: again 100 students.

Drawing

A third subject which can be taught effectively to a large group is drawing. Since the process by which drawing is learned consists of ninety percent personal concentration and involvement with not more than 10 percent instruction, this is another course which is absurdly and inefficiently taught in small classes. It seems almost phenomenal that nowhere in the country can one find a high school drawing class of one hundred students. The only drawing course which is offered in most high schools is mechanically drawing, and for some reason this subject is invariably taught in small classes.

The Technology of Large Group Instruction

All large group instructional rooms should be outfitted with equipment especially designed for the teaching of large groups. A transistorized microphone which does not require a connecting cord to the amplifier is essential. This instrument is worn around the neck of the instructor. With this type of equipment, the teacher can range easily about the room with no concern about tripping over connecting cords. The teacher's voice is amplified through loudspeakers. The overhead projector is especially suitable for large group instruction. This innovation more than any other is responsible for increasing class size to a minimum of 60 or more students.

Modular Scheduling a Gold Plated Fad

Education in the 1960's has become afflicted by fadism. A fad which has attracted considerable attention is varying the length of class time in such an extreme fashion that a student cannot be scheduled without a computer. The enormous amount of money which the largesse of foundations is investing in modular scheduling makes this a gold plated fad. There is very little reason for having the length of the class vary from day to day. Except for an occasional longer period for science labs, changing the length of a class from day to day is just so much busy-work. The effort to carry on this activity greatly increases the housekeeping duties of principals already overburdened with custodial activities.

Perhaps the best evidence of the unimportance of varying

class time from day to day is seen in the fact that colleges and universities make absolutely no effort to do this. Colleges obviously do not shy away from modular scheduling because it would be difficult for them to do. The college schedule would be a natural for this, yet higher education ignores it. I find it extremely paradoxical that Stanford University, which has received hundreds of thousands of dollars of foundation funds to fluctuate the length of class time at the secondary school level, is not the least bit interested in this application on the Stanford campus. This is another case of the public schools being victimized by theoreticians in the colleges of education. Hundreds of thousands of dollars is very expensive "tinkering."

The planning of class time is hardly complex enough to require professional time-study experts to construct schedules. If a school is interested in varying its time schedule, the formula is simple. Most schools have a six-period day and the student is scheduled for six periods. An example of easy variance with no computer required is:

Monday	*Tuesday*	*Wednesday*	*Thursday*	*Friday*
Students meet classes 1 thru 6.	Students meet only classes 1, 3, 5.	Students meet classes 2, 4, 6.	Students meet classes 1 thru 6.	Students meet classes 1 thru 6.

On Monday, Thursday, and Friday students attend six classes, each of which is one hour in length. On Tuesday and Wednesday students meet only three classes and these are two hours in length. This arrangement affords a double class for all disciplines one day a week, which adequately takes care of the need for longer periods for science laboratories.

Chapter Eight

THE LIBRARY IN THE

MULTIPHASED SCHOOL

The multiphased process of education is having a needed effect upon the library of the school. The dynamics of individual learning, and its motivation of students, are making demands that the traditional library cannot meet.

The Conventional School Library (An Educational Disaster)

In the traditional school, librarians have deliberately made the library a place of intricacy and mystery. They have cultivated an esoteric atmosphere calculated to make the school library a dormant, little used, sanctified place. In this setting teachers are so bewildered and frustrated that, as often as not, they sell their programs short rather than attempt to schedule classes in the library. In short, the school library has failed to function as a major service to the classroom. In most schools the library is operated as an autonomous center, responsible to the administration of the school rather than to the needs of students and teachers. Limitations imposed by school librarians are so severe and autocratic that they hinder and restrict the use of what should be a cultural center.

A classic example of the bottleneck imposed by librarians is the practice in most schools of closing the library several weeks before school ends in order for the librarian to take inventory. Many school librarians also keep the library closed in the fall after school opens, for their convenience in shelving new materials. While the schools operate for nine months, they receive no more than eight months of library service. The effects of the librarians' tactics are seen in the negative achievements of the school library. For instance, one rarely hears of a school library which is open in the evening—yet many schools are staffed by more than one librarian and this could easily be managed. Here we are, in an era in which the gross supply of knowledge is being doubled every ten years, and the knowledge centers of the schools continue to close and lock their doors at 3:00 P.M. The librarian profession, it would seem, is simply not a service-oriented occupation.

The attitude of school librarians toward restricted use of the library is reflected in the story of the superintendent who greeted his librarians with the words: "Good morning, Mrs. Smith, and how are things with you today?" "Never better," was the lady's reply. "Do you know, there are only three books out."

The image which students hold of their school library was succinctly expressed by an incident which happened in a school that I visited recently. This school had formerly used the services of two librarians but had released one librarian about six months prior to my visit. In an effort to increase service to students the displaced librarian had been replaced with an English teacher whose instructions were to "run her legs off for students and teachers." My visit to this school occurred several months after this unique arrangement had been set up. Curious about the effectiveness of the *teacher in the library*, I inquired of a serious-looking student whether she would prefer having another librarian working in the place of this teacher, who was called a "director of research." Her classic response was: "Oh, no, Mr. Brown, another librarian would be so busy being a librarian that she wouldn't be able to help anybody." The new library person must be a "director of learning" who is indeed willing to "run her legs off for teachers and students." Service should be the central theme in the training of librarians. In the past this concept has been largely ignored.

The Problem of the Encyclopedia

The physical presence of disapproving librarians is not the only obstacle to increased use of the library. Librarians have surrounded themselves with other stumbling blocks. Most school libraries with modest budgets are weak because of the over-emphasis on owning encyclopedias. A major strategy of encyclopedia publishing houses is to maintain an energetic, aggressive, and determined force of sales people, who have made librarians a prime target and call upon them regularly. The result is that many school libraries purchase new sets of encyclopedias annually, at the expense of not equipping their libraries with other books. Publishers of other books do most of their contacting by mail. This is meager competition for the vigorous sales pitches of reference book salesmen. The result is that school libraries are kept in subjugation to encyclopedia publishing houses with a consequent over-owning and over-use of encyclopedias in the schools.

Not long ago the Executive Secretary of the American Library Association of the National Education Association, smarting from my criticism of school libraries in a recent book, sent me a collection of pamphlets about library operation. I was appalled to discover that of the half dozen pamphlets sent, five of them had been published by encyclopedia publishing houses. Now, encyclopedia publishers are not deeply or even remotely interested in school libraries. They are in the same business as the Yale Lock Company—selling. It is surprising indeed that they have attained a quasi-official status with the American Library Association. No wonder we have an over-emphasis on the owning of reference books in school libraries. School libraries should either minimize or eliminate entirely encyclopedias.

While not nearly enough people have concerned themselves with the dreadful encyclopedia problem, I find a kindred spirit in my friend Martin Mayer. Mayer, who is generally considered to be one of the ablest and best-informed writers on the educational scene, had this to say about the use of encyclopedias in a recent talk:

> Another thing that has bothered me is the emphasis on the reference collection. I have nothing against reference collections. I do not use them much. A salesman sent me a set recently which was very nice of him, and I have had occasion to look at it in the privacy of my own home. It is not very accurate in the areas where I know something. I gather from people whom I have consulted that none of them is terribly accurate in any area in which somebody knows something. And I have since run into people who write articles for encyclopedias. Poor ink-stained wretches right out of *Bartleby the Scrivener*. This is the lowest form of writing in life, and the worst way to try to make a living in this world is to turn out stuff for encyclopedias at 2¢ a word, out of secondary source

material, none of which you check, and then the encyclopedia publisher goes and gets a big name by putting a couple of initials on the thing. And all over the schools we are pushing kids to read this stuff, which is not well written, which is not usefully arranged very often, and which is moreover on its basic level not always very accurate. It is also, incidentally, despite the bias for contemporary, very often out of date. I thought we were going to get a big benefit out of the $64,000 Question and "21" and the blow-up that followed. I felt certain that we would stop thinking it was quite so important to have memorized some encyclopedia. But we do not seem to have won on that. This is still regarded as a really good way to get information for a report and I would love to see some pressure put on by librarians against this notion.

If the encyclopedia in a school library is five years old, and there is $300 in the budget, it might be better to spend the $300 for books and let the encyclopedia go a little longer. It is not up to date anyway. They don't change that much of it every time around.

The major deterrent to student research and individual study is the encyclopedia—yet the encyclopedia continues to be the best stocked item in the school library. As a medium for learning, the encyclopedia reports factually on assimilated data. As an instrument of research, it is a straw in the wind. In the face of complete inadequacy, the encyclopedia remains the chief soure of information in most school libraries. To correct this situation, it is recommended that the encyclopedias be taken off the library shelves before school opens in the fall. Several months after school has been underway, and when students are not around, they may be slipped quietly back onto the shelves. In the meantime, students will have been weaned away from them and will have discovered better and more original sources of information.

Students must learn to use a library without an encyclopedia in it. They must be taught to analyze important and erudite monographs weighted with conflicting opinion. They must be exposed to interpretive study. They must learn that there are always more questions than there are answers, but that a quest for questions and for answers is exciting, vital, and worthy of a life's dedication. We must set our sights high, and if we fail, fail honestly.

A New Type of Librarian Is Needed

The encyclopedia is by no means the only suffocating influence in the school library. Its dominance has assumed such proportions that it is easily the most obvious problem, but school libraries simply abound with discomfiting controls. I know of one junior high library which has practically no books but does have a telephone. One hundred dollars a year for badly needed books is being plowed into the conversational pleasures of the librarian. When I inquired of the administration of this school as to the number of calls the librarian might make in a day and to whom the calls would be placed, I was informed that this was none of my business.

One of the major problems with the position of school librarian is the fact that the job has not been attractive enough to interest brilliant and creative people. Librarian training is comprised of a vast collection of minutia administered by professors of education. The combination of trivia, taught in a setting of sterility, is more than creative minds can bear. The result is that most school library positions must be filled from the ranks of people whose training has been narrow, obstinate, and deeply steeped in irrelevant detail.

The Rebellion in the Library

School libraries have not been nearly what they should be, and the situation is no longer tolerable. Both teachers and students are in open rebellion against library restrictions and are demanding much more from school libraries than they have received in the past. The library situation is illustrated by the action of students at Dickinson College who instituted extreme

measures in a recent effort to do something about the hours
when their library was available. The Dickinson story is told
in a release from the Office of Information Services of the
College which reported on the incident:

> Backing up their petition with a sit-in, Dickinson College
> students have won a fight for longer library hours. Fifty stu-
> dents refused to leave the library when lights went out at the
> 9:45 p.m. closing time recently. "They were polite and good-
> natured but adamant" reported Professor Nancy Loughridge,
> the acting librarian. The 45 minute demonstration was en-
> gineered by the Student Senate in a move to get the li-
> brary staff to reconsider student petitions for longer hours.
> Students wanted the library to open an hour earlier and close
> an hour later. They also wanted the reserve rooms open over
> the lunch and dinner hours and longer Sunday hours.
>
> The library in opposing the petitions contended its budget
> did not permit expansion of the staff to take care of the extra
> hours. But the sit-in carried the day.
>
> Now the Dickinson library opens at 8:30 a.m., closes at
> 10:45 p.m. Reserves and other restricted-use rooms are open
> whenever the library is open. The new library week is 93½
> hours and the budget is up $100 a month.
>
> Professor Loughridge says that as enrollment mounts in
> the colleges, students are using libraries more and more for
> study in order to escape the distractions of crowded dormi-
> tories.
>
> Formerly, students studied in their rooms and used li-
> braries mostly for collateral reading and research. Dickinson's
> proposed new library will have carrels for all of its students,
> Professor Loughridge said.[1]

The Materials Center Concept

A number of school leaders are advocating that the concept
of the school library as a place containing books be changed to
what is popularly called a "materials center." This is nonsense.
What a knowledge-centered school needs is a first class library

---

[1] Office of Information Services, Dickinson College, Carlisle, Pennsylvania,
January 21, 1964.

made up of the best collection of books the school and community can afford. The idea of a materials center was discussed effectively in the publication of the Association for Supervision and Curriculum Development. The issue was stated so clearly that it is being reprinted here.

> A Library is a Library. Make it a Materials Center and you have created something else. Put it in an All-Purpose Room and you have changed its purpose. Divide it up among classrooms and you have altered its function. A library is a place for books. And books need people to enjoy them. Children to pore over them, to wander through them, to leaf over them and laugh over them and love them. Teachers to know them, to delight in them, and to want to share them. Librarians who are not merely keepers but the ambassadors of books, their representatives, their introducers, their friends and advocates . . . A library that sees itself as a Materials Center looks in a different way at a book. I do not believe that books can be relegated to the region of materials, touching as many of them do on the realm of the heart and the spirit. . . .[2]

Education by Appointment

In nongraded schools with multiphased curricula, increasing numbers of students are assuming responsibility for some aspects of their education. This responsibility often takes the form of independent study punctuated with teacher appointments. The library is the most logical place for students in individual programs to be based. Their studies call for materials of such extreme variegation that their work cannot be adequately accommodated any other place. These students do not place an additional burden on library service. They have acquired a sophisticated approach to the learning process which allows them to go about their business in an efficient, orderly, and independent fashion.

---

[2] Isabel Wilner, Librarian, Lida Lee Tall School, Towson State College, Baltimore, Maryland, in *Educational Leadership,* January, 1964.

Unfortunately, there are still many people in the schools who are opposed to releasing high school students from the classroom for the purpose of undertaking independent research. These people still look upon research as a process which should be restricted to graduate schools. If they could just capture the spirit of research advocated by C. F. Kettering, who claimed:

> Research is a high-hat word that scares a lot of people. It needn't. It is nothing but a state of mind—a friendly, welcoming attitude toward change. It is the problem-solving mind as contrasted with the let-well-enough-alone mind. It is the composed mind instead of the fiddler mind. It is the tomorrow mind instead of the yesterday mind.

A graphic illustration of what happens when students are allowed intellectual freedom made national headlines several years ago. When a reporter from *Time* magazine telephoned the superintendent of a small New England high school to inquire how it happened that among 24,000 contestants in the Westinghouse Science Talent Search, this one high school produced students who won both first and second place, the reply of the superintendent was revealing. "Both of the students were bright and the school got out of their way." One of the best ways for the school to get out of the way of its bright students is to multiphase the curriculum and arrange for their unlimited use of the library. What is the role of the library in a school whose multiphased curriculum dynamically reflects the influences of modern science and technology?

Recommendations for the Library in the Multiphased School

Recommendation 1 The library should be enlarged or a new one constructed to seat increasing numbers of students. The modern junior or senior high school library should accommodate at least 25 percent of the student body at any one time. The modern elementary school library should accommodate no less than 20 percent of its student body at one time.

Recommendation 2   The rectangular tables in the school library, which accommodate from four to eight students at a table, should be replaced with carrels. To expect students to concentrate and study in a hotel lobby atmosphere at an age when body chemistry has juices jangling at an abnormal rate is an incredible absurdity. Individual study carrels must be provided for every student.

Recommendation 3   A dictionary and a synonym-finder or Thesaurus must be furnished for each carrel. Students will be more inclined to use these items if they are readily available and do not require an interruption and a walk across the room.

Recommendation 4   The library in all new schools must be located close to the street so that it is readily accessible during the afternoon and evening when the rest of the school is closed.

Recommendation 5   The renovation of the library should separate the charge-out desk from the reading room. This is a noise factor which must be eliminated. The best arrangement is a lobby containing the librarian and the business of the library. The reading room should be reserved for students and books.

Recommendation 6   At least 20 percent of the cost of any new school should be spent in building and equipping the school library. There should be available a minimum of twelve books per student.

Recommendation 7   There must be small rooms six feet by six feet with typewriters and tape recorders available for individual student activity.

Recommendation 8   The school library should be carpeted for sound privacy and air conditioned for comfort. While we are not endorsing air conditioned schools, air conditioning serves a special purpose in the library. The library should contain many small rooms where students can use technical aids in comfort and privacy. Without the air conditioning these rooms will be uncomfortable.

Recommendation 9   School librarians should be required to have teaching experience. Certification requirements universally require all other professional non-teaching personnel to have teaching experience. This is considered basic for counselors and administrators. It is equally important that librarians have this experience.

Recommendation 10   One trained librarian is quite enough for any library. Additional personnel should be clerks whose chief function is one of friendly assistance. These personnel must be willing to go to extremes in their efforts to assist students in the pursuit of knowledge.

Recommendation 11   Libraries should be open after school and in the evening for student and teacher use. If this facility is properly equipped, it is absurd for it to be open only during school hours.

Recommendation 12   Community memberships should be welcomed in school libraries.

Recommendation 13   Librarians should not be permitted to impose upon teachers the chores of collecting fines and getting books returned. Asking teachers to hold up reports cards for library business should not be permitted.

Summary

School administrators in charge of traditional school buildings should not refrain from moving into a multiphased kind of education simply because they are handicapped by a conventionally constructed school plant. Melbourne High School, which invented the concept of a nongraded high school, is housed in an old, very conventionally constructed plant. The school was nongraded for five years before any additional buildings were constructed to fit into the new curriculum concept. When a multiphased school does have the opportunity for expansion it should be in the direction of a new library. An old library is easily converted into classroom space so there is no loss of plant use when it is abandoned.

The school's new library should be a place of intellectual excitement and the design should incorporate the recommendations contained in this chapter. The new library should ideally be a building by itself located near the street in order that it is easily accessible after school and in the evenings. This will also make it convenient for community use.

Through the cooperation of the Educational Facilities Laboratories of the Ford Foundation, I am including on pages 44 and 45, six imaginative designs for new school libraries. The emphasis of the new library building must be on bigness and uniqueness of design to accommodate a growing number of students interested in independent study and research. The library must be as large as the gymnasium. Its function is vastly more important.

As the concept of students receiving their education by appointment becomes more highly developed, more and more students will take advantage of this exciting and more fulfilling way of learning. We may soon be constructing new high schools which will eventually become libraries and research centers as students become increasingly involved in this new venture in education.

Chapter Nine

A NEW CURRICULUM

FOR DROPOUTS

The Second Industrial Revolution

It is already past time for the educational system to pause and consider the effects of a wildly automating industry on the lives of students now being educated for the future world of work. Further disregard of the effects of automation may well be calamitous.

John Diebold, one of the brightest of the young prophets in the new field of automation, predicted recently that within the next few years the employment of sixty million Americans is "practically certain to be obsolete." Senator Jennings Randolph of West Virginia, a member of the Senate Employment Security Committee, estimates that automation and technological improvement will bring about a loss of four million jobs in the next twelve months alone. When we add to this astounding figure the 1,350,000 new jobs needed by young people coming into the labor market every year, then the employment prospects for boys and girls now in the public schools appear to be dim. Representative William Fitts Ryan, D., N.Y., has called for a congressional study of what he calls an "economic revolution" caused by automation forcing men to give way to automated production lines and electronic brains. John L. Snyder, Jr., head of one of the multi-million-dollar companies which makes automation equipment, advises that machines are now replacing men at the rate of 40,000 jobs a week.

Another dimension to the problem of automation is seen when we examine the matter of a constantly decreasing work week. Between 1900 and 1940 technological improvements reduced the length of the work week by twenty hours as the sixty-hour week was shortened to a forty-hour week. President George Meany of the AFL-CIO recently called for a "thirty-five hour week or less now, and later on God only knows how short it will have to be." It is becoming increasingly evident that within the forseeable future all of the goods and services needed by our economy may be produced by as little as three or four percent of the nation's total work force. The rapid outpouring of technological discoveries has reached such an amazing pace that the impact of invention on the future of students now in school simply staggers the imagination.

A Society of Leisure

The implications for education are just beginning to emerge. By 1975 computerized technology will have forced the nation to begin the sociological change from a world of work to a world of leisure. Surprisingly, the very suggestion of a world of "no work" instinctively shocks the educational profession. Our present society has been so schooled in the work ethic that the proposal to change to an ethic of no work is swiftly and positively repelled. Inherent in this reaction against a life of leisure and a "no work" ethic is the Puritan belief on which the country was built. In essence, idleness is a sin and morality is synonomous with hard work.

In the 1960's the unemployed no longer starve. By the 1970's we will have become adjusted to the idea that leisure is a virtue. What kind of education will be needed by individuals living in a society of little work? Individuals in the schools must have a far more rigorous basic education than they now receive. Since the economy of the future will provide substantial blocks of disposable leisure for all persons, then Americans must begin the search for another fulfillment. This can be found only in education. In essence, if an individual is to experience self-fulfillment to a high degree, then he must be equipped with highly developed skills for learning. We have long known that the good life is an intellectual life. The new society created by technological advances must provide exciting intellectual expression for its members, all of whom will have substantial amounts of free time. This will give dimensions to our society that other societies have not had. In this highly technological setting it is incumbent upon the schools to do much more for the vast army of the uneducated. The massive encroachment of automation has so severely disturbed the economy that it will take a radically different education to restore balance.

DROPOUTS, PUSHOUTS AND DROPINS

Through the advances in industrial technology unskilled jobs are being rapidly eliminated. The process is bringing to the fore a "dropout" problem which is approaching a national scandal. Last year between thirty and forty percent of all teenage youngsters dropped straight out of school and into the vanishing market of unskilled jobs. We can no longer afford or tolerate this problem.

What is a school dropout? The best definition of a dropout is a person of school age who leaves school before he has prepared himself for work consistent with his intellectual capacity. In a recent study of 2,400 dropouts made by the Colorado State Department of Education it was found that more than 60 percent of the high school dropouts were average or above average in ability, but nearly 70 percent were below average in scholastic achievement. Another significant factor reported by the survey was that 40 percent of the dropouts had been retained in one or more grades in school.

Unfortunately the schools have no conception of how to cope with the dropout, for he cannot be absorbed into the existing system of education. Many schools are actually glad to see the dropout leave school. Others are, at best, ambivalent about his departure. This is the chance to get rid of a prickly pear. It is indeed unfortunate that the agencies which accredit schools do not ask to see the school's dropout reports.

Dropins

Last September, after much Presidential exhortation, thousands of dropouts returned to high school. The whole operation was absurd. The schools failed to make changes in their curriculum to meet the needs of these returning students, so what happened? Dropouts were brought back to the same uncompromising learning situation which they had left. According to the Associated Press, two weeks after school started, 90 percent of the returnees had dropped out again and the schools were once more confronted with a continually embarrassing distraction. So, through Presidential intervention, we have created a new problem—one which can be described as the "dropin."

Our proclivity for locking the barn door after the horse has been stolen is seen in the recent legislation proposed in Congress to pay potential dropouts $20 a week to stay in school. With tongue in cheek, I am tempted to suggest that a more effective device would be to give all potential dropouts motor-scooters as an incentive to keep them in school. The school could maintain the title to the scooter which might be presented to the "salvaged" dropout along with his diploma. The appeal would be enormous! But, quite seriously, I am afraid that the current national interest in dropouts is not based on any genuine concern for their welfare but rather on the fact that they are a source of unrelieved irritation. The really big problem facing society is what to do about the idle high school leaver. He has lost all sense of direction, if indeed he ever had any.

New Curricula Needed

We must plan curricula especially for early school leavers with the same diligence that we prepare programs for the gifted. It is to our national discredit that every single one of the curriculum improvement projects sponsored by the National Science Foundation has been designed for the student whose achievement is average or above. William H. Bristow, an Assistant Superintendent in New York City, supported the idea of a special curriculum linked to the needs of potential dropouts recently when he wrote:

> We need a new rationale for curriculum for that con-
> siderable segment of the school population variously classified
> as non-learners, reluctant learners, slow learners, potential
> dropouts—a rationale which will square with their needs and
> needs of culture.

The dropout problem is not just a continually embarrassing distraction—it is a highly complex educational problem. Consequently, whatever we do, we must be careful that there are no depreciatory overtones. We must make classes in basic skills as important and honorable as accelerated classes in academic subjects.

What is an appropriate education for the dropout? One which seeks to discover and cultivate individual strengths and potentialities. The education of the potential dropout must no longer be based on conformity. It must be variegated enough to appeal to unique weaknesses and strengths. Their action in taking the frightening step of leaving school is proof enough that their minds will not tolerate the pedantic, the illogical, and the ineffective. School leavers have been frustrated and discouraged by a curriculum that is narrow, repetitious, unimaginative and far from first rate.

Pushouts

One important dimension to the dropout problem is the fact that many students are literally *pushed* out of school. It would be interesting indeed if we could gather statistics that would show the percentage of dropouts who are really "pushouts." The numbers which respond to a push from the school somehow manage not to get recorded.

Most of the difficulties of students are rooted in the obsolescence of graded curricula. Not being able to endure a system which does not fit, each individual escapes in his own way. Can we really condemn children who escape out of the cage of the graded school into truancy and the world of fantasy and daydreams? Can we blame even the student who stays in school but drops out psychologically because of boredom? If attending school is to be a compulsory obligation, we must assure ourselves that it does more good than it does harm.

In the National Interest

There is currently much national ado about physical fitness. Such headlines as "Crash Physical Testing Ordered for Youths" are appearing regularly in newspapers around the country. It must be strongly emphasized that the President's program on physical fitness has embraced mental fitness as well. The reason for this is obvious. The physical unfitness problem is minor compared to the mental unfitness caused by poor education and the dropout problem. The manner in which national reports have lumped the physical and mental problems of youth together is seen in the following U.P.I. release:

> Johnson City, Tex. (U.P.I.) Alarmed by the physical, mental and moral deficiencies of thousands of young American men, President Johnson announced that pre-induction draft examinations will be given as soon as possible to all eligible 18 year old males.
>
> . . . What motivated Johnson's action was a report from a special task force on manpower conservation set up last September by the late President John F. Kennedy. The task force was headed by Labor Secretary W. Willard Wirtz who presented the report to Johnson at his ranch here Friday.
>
> Of 306,000 young men reported for pre-induction examination in 1962, 152,000 or 49.8 per cent were disqualified.
>
> "These youths were found lacking in the physical, mental or moral equipment considered essential to absorb military training and to perform satisfactorily in our modern armed forces," the report said. It seemed evident that many of these individuals would be equally handicapped in finding acceptance in the civilian labor market of the 1960's.
>
> Wirtz said findings of the task force also indicated that for the rejectees it probably means that they are going to have a very hard time of it for the rest of their lives.

It is becoming increasingly evident that many more youths are failing to meet minimal mental achievement standards than minimum physical health standards. Also, the President blames poverty as the principal reason why so many youths fail to meet army induction standards, and this indeed contributes to the problem.

One of the first major learning handicaps which the potential dropout must overcome is poorly developed language habits. Early speech patterns acquired in the home and neighborhood increase the disadvantage of the already disadvantaged youngster. The poor speech and expressive habits which disadvantaged youngsters absorb from their surroundings give them a sorry base for reading instruction in phonics.

Graded Education Must Go

Walter H. Bristow, the Assistant Superintendent for the New York City School Board I mentioned earlier, succinctly described the major issue in a paper on the dropout problem: "Grade standards no longer have validity in the face of research in the growth and development patterns of children." The solution to the dropout problem lies in the philosophy of nongraded education, which realigns youngsters on the basis of achievement and permits each to develop to his highest potential. Every school must offer a broad, flexible program designed to meet individual differences. There is nothing so unequal as the equal treatment of unequals.

THE SCHOOL'S RESPONSIBILITY FOR DROPOUTS

The school is the only organization in society which comes into contact with all children; from this it derives enormous responsibility. The heads of school systems must not rest until the needs of all youngsters have been met. The schools have long paid close attention to the culturally advantaged. The position of these children's parents in the power structure of the community has kept school administrators alert to their needs, and the result is that ceilings have been removed from their opportunities.

The position of the potential dropout is reversed. School administrators have not been concerned with a low ceiling. The problem here is that the school has too often asked of this youngster what he could not do. The potential dropout is usually unable to express his frustration to school people, and his parents are not significant in the power structure of the community. The result is a highly complex and embarrassing school-leaving problem. Nearly all school leavers are reluctant to drop from the school's rolls. The step is a frightening one to which they have been driven by inappropriate curricula and teachers who have failed to understand their problems. When a school designs curricula suited to the needs of each individual, the dropout problem will disappear.

Most of the problems of early school leavers center around their failure to learn. This may be caused by a variety of factors. A curriculum designed to eliminate gaps in learning is essential if we are to come to grips with the dropout problem. The following proposals were written by a teacher who spends her entire school time working on special curricula for early school leavers:

> Before one can attempt to design an effective high school program for the so-called low-achiever, the very term itself and the implications it carries must be carefully examined. Students who fall into the category of non-learners are diverse in nature, ability, background, and personality. Their one common characteristic lies in the fact that they have progressed up the educational ladder to a particular point in high school —yet their achievement as measured by past records, marks, test scores, and teacher evaluations shows them to be considerably below the achievement level of the high school student.
>
> In a conventional high school large groups of non-learners reach the front door of the school, are distributed into heterogeneous classes of students some of which are achieving at a much faster rate, and are confronted with the same indifferent treatment to which they have become accustomed. The usual disregard of the needs of these students consists of giving them the same materials, occasionally in a watered-down form, treating them as the "slow" ones in the class, and doing nothing more than letting them lag further and further behind. At the end of three, four, five, or more years, these reluctant learners will be graduated or will have dropped out of school and their

high school careers will be ended. Where they go from this point and what they do is no longer the concern of the school —furthermore, there is a whole fresh new batch of low-achievers for the school to deal with in the same insensitive fashion.

Perhaps this commentary appears a little harsh. Maybe a great many traditional high schools do attempt to provide for these students in a slightly more sympathetic manner. Nevertheless, the implication is clear; with the advent of Sputnik, the stepped-up atomic age, and the vital need for high caliber brain-power, the low-achiever has been shoved, coerced, and directed further and further into the background. During the same interval the high achiever has come boldly to the forefront as the potential savior of America in her troubled times.

Since we are basically a moralistic society, educators dotted here and there have combined practicality and idealism in equal parts, the plight of the low-achiever has been noticed, discussed, and deplored.

The first step toward a sensible solution lies in setting up special classes for reluctant learners. Homogeneity in the classroom is difficult to achieve, but a large number of slow learners may be easily spotted and grouped together in classes which are coupled to their individual needs. Granted, once the low classes are formed, the next problem which arises is one of obtaining a staff of teachers who are both willing and capable of working with these students. The teachers who deal with the low-achievers must be unique in several respects. First of all, they must be enthusiastic about the somewhat formidable task which confronts them; the task of delivering learning to the student who has not been a good producer in the past. Secondly, the teachers who elect and are chosen to work with modest learners must be flexible and experimentally minded, for this is a field where few educational theories or concepts are either satisfactory or useful.

Now the stage is partly set. The teachers are chosen and the students are grouped. The next barrier is a practical one— the problem of facilities. All physical situations vary, but the low-achiever probably is more influenced by facilities than any other group of students. Low-achievers delight in easy chairs, informal classroom arrangements, excellent lighting, air-conditioning, quiet, and other luxuries conducive to study. The use of study carrels rather than conventional desks is a decided asset in teaching these youngsters.

When physical needs are met, the next problem is one of materials. It is absurd to assume that the usual state-adopted textbooks are satisfactory for students with serious learning problems. The conscientious teacher of the disadvantaged learner must probe far beyond a state textbook program in the search for suitable educational materials. The ability levels of low-achievers must be carefully assessed and materials provided for variances in achievement. Needless to say, the more materials of the right type, the easier the task of implementing this program. Materials and books for low-achieving students are expensive; money is probably scarce, but scrimping on materials will cause the downfall of the program even before it has begun.

Funds must be spent for materials for these youngsters with the same abandon it has been spent for materials for the talented. Once all of these aforementioned problems have been met and solved satisfactorily, the next mission is to define the goals in the program for the low-achiever. This goal can only be stated in the basic premise—"to develop the student to his highest potential, always considering his talents (however limited), and to take a student where he is and help him to grow." This is rather a general statement, but its implications are significant.

Low-achievers are sometimes, though not always, limited in their ability to develop intellectually. The problem is that they are at a low level in what they have achieved in the past and their educational foundations are terribly weak. Progress will never be revolutionary nor fast and the goals of the program should not imply immediate success. Education of the reluctant learner is more of a developmental than an educational program.

The next area which should be examined is the important issue of how to deal with the classroom atmosphere. The climate of the classroom is largely teacher-created and its importance in the program for the low-achiever cannot be over-stressed. For these frequently tense, frustrated and highly nervous students, the environment of the classroom must be informal, relaxed, and at times, almost permissive. The low ability student must never feel teacher-induced stress. Such stress will usually cause him to stop working and either sit and do nothing, or contribute to disorder in a general way. High-achievers respond to the pressure of marks by assimilating more knowledge; low-achievers frequently respond to the adversity of their marks with apathy and lessened productivity. The teacher of the low-achievers must be prepared to meet students at very low levels of performance and then utilize every possible method in building desirable classroom atmosphere where these students can and will learn.

Rapport—what a lovely word, and yet can it ever be established with the low-achiever? Consider the point at which these students enter high school. They have probably been laughed at too many times, they have probably been openly chastized by teachers on occasions too numerous to count. So, is it any wonder that the low-achiever does not welcome discussion classes and indeed appears disinterested, uncaring, and unmotivated at the very mention of classroom discussion? And yet this need not be the case. The teacher who is willing to develop a strategy and use every possible psychological device, can and does finally establish a permissive give-and-take atmosphere between herself and her group of low-achievers. The right environment contributes vitally to learning.

The establishment of satisfactory rapport is one of the most challenging issues to confront the teacher of the low-achiever. The very diversity of this group of students serves to intensify this problem. Low-achieving students must develop the willingness to contribute, discuss, and ask questions in class. No learning situation is satisfactory without these components.

A major stumbling block confronting teachers is that many low-achieving students are emotionally unstable. In order to preserve and encourage harmonious relations in the classroom with low-achievers the teacher must act as a stabilizer and not as a disciplinarian.

Along with the problem of classroom atmosphere comes the never-ending chore of classroom routine and procedures for the low-achieving student. These students are quickly bored by routine, consequently a minimum of time and effort should be spent on the usual treadmill type of activity. Surprisingly and pleasingly, these students do appreciate and admire orderliness and organization on the part of the teacher.

Low-achievers offer the best possible candidates for discipline problems within the whole school. Yet, given the right type of program, the discipline problems for this group become nonexistent.

Low-achievers are accustomed to failure and lack of success. Their program must be organized so that they see and feel progress and success. Collectively these students are by no means intellectually incompetent. At worse, some are true slow learners, who would test quite low in general achievement. At best some are students who have never been motivated to learn and who consequently have reached high school without learning very much. The teacher must realize and recognize these problems for what they are and deal with them appropriately. The teacher of the low-achievers must never teach down to her students; nor should she assume that she is the all-knowing salvation for the low-achiever. This work need be neither altrusitic nor sacrificial. Instead it is rewarding and satisfying teaching. It is stimulating in the highest degree.

Motivation and the instilling of the desire to learn: perhaps these are the paramount tasks of the teacher of the low-achiever. Once the low-achiever is sincerely motivated to learn, a great deal can be accomplished. It is important for the teacher to remember that the factor of motivation is not a static force which can be acquired at the beginning of school and drawn upon from then on. Instead it is a conscious day-by-day task to be faced realistically. The teacher of the low-achiever will probably abandon many conventional teaching methods and devise techniques more likely to get results. Activities in the classroom must be varied as much as is possible. Boredom results in disinterest, serious discipline problems, and leaving school.

Another responsibility which the teacher of the low-achiever must accept is one of building study habits. These students have never known what study habits are. Consequently the teacher must spend considerable time enforcing rigorous requirements designed to equip these students with good study habits. These students need to learn how to learn and, trite as it may sound, this is the most difficult skill to teach." [1]

When the dropout problem is finally solved it will have to be in a nongraded school. It can never be solved in the citadel of routine which is created by graded education. The nongraded organization with its multiphase classes has accomplished miracles in keeping youngsters in school.

Three basic principles stand out as major inhibitors to leaving school: curriculum maneuvers which provide small classes and personal attention; the assignment of talented teachers to this program; and the offering of curricula linked to the rate of learning of each individual.

---

[1] "Recommendations for an Effective Program for Early School Leavers." Presented to the Faculty of Melbourne High School by Louise Bone of the English Department. January, 1965.

Chapter Ten

THE DISADVANTAGED STUDENT

AND THE NONGRADED PROCESS

After fifty years of compulsory education the United States is still confronted with vast numbers of adults who have received little or no education. The dilemma is compounded by the fact that roughly one third of the students currently in school are not being adequately educated. The major issue facing the United States in the sixties is what to do about the uneducated. This is the major factor underlying President Johnson's "Pockets of Poverty Program."

One of the leading spokesmen for better education for the culturally deprived is Agnes Meyer, Chairman of the National

Committee for Support of the Public Schools. Last year at the first national conference of this organization, Mrs. Meyer vigorously called for improved education for the disadvantaged youngster:

> . . . We are involved in a second Industrial Revolution that will be more severe, more agonizing, more complex than the first Industrial Revolution, which gave us Karl Marx, unless it is accompanied by an educational revolution geared to the needs of today.
>
> . . . Unless we are prepared to write off our great masses of illiterate and untrained, we must hasten their preparation for a productive life in our technological society through education, or put them permanently on relief.
>
> . . . The answer to unemployment, automation, delinquency, economic stagnation, is a first-rate school system.

And, speaking before the National Conference of Industrial Leaders last year, Mrs. Meyer pointed up the rather frightening alternatives to success in educating the large masses of people.

> . . . Furthermore, if we continue to neglect the education of millions of our citizens, we are in danger of becoming not one but two nations in our automated society—the one educated and affluent which will have to support the illiterate and impoverished on the dole. We are faced with the menace of a permanent underclass. Even now the failure to educate results in an appalling expenditure for relief. The U.S. Assistant Secretary of H.E.W. testified before a Congressional committee in 1962, there are 7¼ million persons in our affluent society receiving welfare payments today. Total annual federal, state, and local expenditures for this purpose exceed 4.5 billion dollars. Forty-five percent of all families with less than $2,000 annual income have a head of family with less than an eighth grade education.
>
> . . . Now you may say that our theme "It pays to educate" sounds too materialistic. Believe me, we are not unaware of the other not less important aspects of better education for all our citizens. In his statesmanlike address to the Congress and

the American people, President Johnson called for an end of the teaching of hate and violence. Much of this hatred and violence is spread by the ignorant who feel that the rapid acceleration of change due to technological progress is sweeping them into the scrapheap.

. . . I ask you to face the fact that our nation is in serious trouble. The heart of the trouble is our sluggish economy. Forty thousand people are thrown out of work every week by automation. "The most important problem in the world today," says the Swedish economist, Gunnar Myrdal, "is that America shall succeed in getting out of the rut of slow economic progress. A nation which cannot solve its own economic problems can scarcely assert the leadership it should have in international affairs."

The search on every hand is for a better way to educate that portion of the population which the schools call by such names as low achievers, handicapped children, culturally different and disadvantaged youngsters. It is in this area in particular that the nongraded school process can make a major contribution. The nongraded school is decidedly not, as many people seem to think, a school which is designed to fit best the needs of the talented. It is highly appropriate to the needs of youngsters with learning problems. The full effect of the nongraded school in the education of the disadvantaged child is clearly seen in the accomplishments of the Nikola Tesla elementary school in Chicago. This school is located in one of the most interesting school districts in the world. The denseness of the population which the school serves is seen in the size of the school district, which is only one block wide and three blocks long. From this area the school draws approximately 900 severely deprived pupils. Roughly 50 percent of the school's parents are on relief and many of the children entering kindergarten are so disadvantaged that they do not even know their own names.

Under the dynamic leadership of Principal Jerome Gilbert, Nikola Tesla has become one of the most successful elementary schools in the world. In achieving this status Principal Gilbert has proved that the nongraded school may well be the solution to the knotty problem of educating disadvantaged children. At my request Dr. Gilbert has prepared a detailed report on this interesting school and its accomplishments. His statement has been reproduced in its entirety.

THE NIKOLA TESLA ELEMENTARY SCHOOL
A Case Study in Nongraded Education

Nokola Tesla School opened as a new kindergarten through sixth grade school in September, 1960. It is located on the south edge of Chicago Public School District Fourteen in the Woodlawn community of Chicago. The boundaries, at that time, were 64th street on the north, Woodlawn Avenue on the west, 67th street on the south, and the Illinois Central Railroad tracks on the east. The Tesla School District, at that time less than nine square blocks in area, was carved out of the two neighboring kindergarten through eighth grade school districts to relieve these schools. Three schools served the Woodlawn area for over one-half century. Between 1953 and 1964, six new schools have been constructed in this area and yet another one is needed.

The neighborhood in which Tesla School is situated developed about a decade after the Columbian Exposition of 1893 which was held about a mile to the north. For the most part, the houses of the community are large apartment buildings that are very overcrowded. Middle-class Negroes who had moved into Woodlawn in the mid-forties have almost entirely been replaced by lower class Negroes. The center of vice and crime in Woodlawn is 63rd Street. Living conditions improve as you go south from 63rd Street.

The Woodlawn community is considered to be one of the most densely populated areas in Chicago. The United States Census "Advanced Table Ph—1. Population and Housing Characteristics: 1960" estimates the total population in District 631 (63rd Street to 67th Street and from Woodlawn Avenue to Kenwood and Dorchester Avenues—an area of twelve blocks) to be 8,284. The Tesla School District included approximately three-fourths of District 631 census tract. Using the three to four ratio, the Tesla School District had a total population of 6,213 of which 1,007 were under five years of age, 574 were from five to nine years old, and 363 children's ages ranged from ten to fourteen years. The pastor of a neighboring Lutheran church stated that he, local politicians, and the Southeast Planning Commission believe that the United States Census Bureau underestimated the population by ten percent. Perhaps some of the census workers wouldn't go into some of those apartment buildings.

The district has not yet reached the saturation point since many buildings between 66th and 67th Streets west of Kenwood Avenue are not yet filled with more than about two families per apartment. As these figures indicate, Tesla School, constructed to hold 660 pupils, became more and more swamped each succeeding year. Tesla opened with about 725 children in September, 1960, and by September 1961, it enrolled over 900 pupils.

The majority of the children of Tesla School come from lower socio-economic class homes. Many of these children come from homes in which the father has left or the mother is remarried or living with another man. Some are illegitimate children. Often the mothers or guardians are employed. In general, these children receive little or improper supervision. Parents show little interest in encouraging the children to succeed in school.

In part, as a consequence of the children's background and of the low value placed upon education by the majority of the parents, the rate of failure of Tesla School children, before the school year 1960–61, had been high. Whereas 14.8% of the first graders failed in District Fourteen as a whole, 19.7% at Tesla School (1960) were retained at this level.

In addition to the difficulties common to primary children everywhere, many lower class children in the district have a meager cultural background. The level of aspirations of their parents are often very low. Many seem satisfied living on public assistance (perhaps about 50%). Since they apparently live for today and show little concern about the future, there is little desire to use education as a means of improving their social or economic position.

Many parents fail to enroll their children in kindergarten at the beginning of the school year, and some fail to register them for kindergarten at all. About one-third of those entering kindergarten are, in fact, only ready for nursery school activities as they often do not even know their own names.

This last fall, two new schools opened. One school took two blocks of children to the west of Tesla School. In October, the other school opened. We sent 550 children to this school and received 450 children from the east of us from two other schools. Our school district is now one block wide and three blocks long. As poor as the children of our old district had been, the children of our new district are even poorer in care and parents' income.

As you can guess, we are really starting our nongraded program all over again. We got our children from schools with relatively strict achievement standards—even failing children in kindergarten. So our nice population is again replaced by large, over-age, hostile, poorly adjusted, and hard to motivate children. We are beginning with a smaller pupil-teacher ratio, however. Previously, classes had from 44 to 47 pupils. Now, our class sizes are down to 33 or 34. As you have noted from the statistics, we raised the reading levels of children significantly in spite of large class sizes, high transiency (we are considered a high transiency school), many emotionally disturbed children, and children from families who do not value education highly. (In spite of what you read in the papers about the reasons for the boycotts, Chicago has excellent schools for all children. In fact, the central part of the city has the newest schools.)

Perhaps you recall that we jumped from 11th place in 1961 to 5th place, in District Fourteen, in the number of children who are reading at their mental age grade expectancy. This was at the third year level and on the basis of the city-wide third grade testing program. We ranked 5th in spite of the fact that our children ranked 13th in the district in terms of reading readiness. Thus, the children coming to us were among the most poorly prepared coming from home to enter the formal school program at the first year level. There are seventeen elementary schools in District Fourteen.

A radically different but equally interesting use of the nongraded process has been reported by the Bureau of Indian Affairs of the U.S. Department of the Interior in the education of Navaho Indians. The education of the Indian who is culturally different is, in many ways, a more difficult problem than the education of the culturally deprived. Both groups are disadvantaged but in different ways. The program involving the Navaho is described as a basic literacy-vocational nongraded program and was first instituted in 1946. The results have been represented by Bureau officials as highly successful. The Bureau is currently interested in a broader application of the nongraded process to all of its schools which deal with children who are culturally different.

It is difficult to understand why educators responsible for teaching in deprived and highly illiterate areas continue to use the graded school as the vehicles for educating disadvantaged youngsters. Anyone with even an elementary knowledge of intellectual differences must recognize the wide range of native ability which exists in children who live in this complex environment. The spread is simply enormous.

Now, what kind of education should deprived youngsters have and how should it be organized? The first objective is to give these children basic literary skills. The second aim is to provide them with vocational or technical skills. In addition to basic literacy and vocational or technical training, they must be helped to develop built-in "second-chance" mechanisms. Because of technological changes wrought by cybernation it is estimated that youngsters in the schools today will have to be retrained at least twice and perhaps three times. These youngsters must acquire a kind of flexibility which will aid them to learn new skills quickly when old skills are automated away.

A School Organized Against Dropouts

How should their education be organized? Since the most important subject for them to learn is reading, from the very beginning between one-half and three-fourths of their school time should be spent directly on this activity or in the related fields of language arts. As the children begin to master the skills of communication this time may be reduced to one-half and eventually to one-third, but no student, deprived or otherwise, should be allowed to spend less than one-third of his time studying reading until such time as he is fluent in this basic subject.

The handicap of a poor start in life is difficult to overcome even when there is no room left at the bottom. Many culturally deprived youngsters are talented in art, music, athletics, and other fields, but because of their deprivation often do not have the opportunity to develop these talents. If we can find a way to improve the education of these youngsters it is possible to salvage both creativity and talent. The child, disadvantaged from cultural deprivation, comes to school with an impoverished language background. He has gross deficiencies in both listening and speaking. Many such youngsters cannot talk coherently and their language is limited to primitive grunts and gestures. In view of the fact that the deprived youngster learns more easily through imitation, the progress of culturally deprived children can be accelerated when it is convenient and possible to have them associate with youngsters from other than deprived homes.

The emphasis on better ways to educate the disadvantaged youngster has centered in the junior and senior high school. The reasons for this are obvious: the problems of disadvantaged youth are far more acute than the problems of disadvantaged children. Disadvantaged adolescents are often in open rebellion against society. More often than not this resistance takes the form of juvenile delinquency, law breaking, and a host of criminal activities. The result has been that this is the age group which has had the most attention paid to its educational needs.

This problem of deprived children should be attacked at its source rather than its place of eruption. In essence, the emphasis on education for the culturally disadvantaged must be shifted from the high school to the nursery schools, kindergarten, and the first grade. Furthermore, an increasing emphasis must be given to the needs of these youngsters in their pre-school years. The whole process calls for a radical departure from the typical approach used by conventionally graded schools. In concentrated areas of deprived children, day nursery schools and child care centers should be established to care for youngsters of whatever age the parents are willing to send them. An unrelenting search must be instituted to find a way to bring *all* children living under conditions of cultural deprivation to these centers by the time they reach their third birthday. Likewise, *all* disadvantaged children must be required to attend kindergarten by the time they are five years old. The conventional graded school has endeavored to absorb disadvantaged children into the learning process as if no differences existed between them and the comfortable children of suburbia. The failure of this system has been monumental and a radical reform of the educational establishment is in order to deal more adequately with the problems of the disadvantaged. This reform must not be with the curricula alone but with state laws which control the age of admission to the public school. The conventional school-entering age of six has the adverse effect of leaving these youngsters too long in their deprived environment.

The Multiphased Kindergarten for the Disadvantaged

All children should not begin school together in September, but attendance should be compulsory beginning with the child's fifth birthday.

Phase 1—Students whose verbal achievement is below the 30th percentile should spend two years in kindergarten.

Phase 2—Students whose verbal achievement is between the 30th and the 40th percentiles spend only one year in kindergarten.

Phase 3—Students whose verbal achievement is above the 50th percentile may enter directly into the primary school.

In addition to the right kind of start for disadvantaged youngsters, the curriculum must also be structured so as to be appropriate to students who come into high school lacking a committment to learning.

An Appropriate Curriculum for Uncommitted Learners

What the nation needs most is a remodeled system of learning designed to accommodate the requirements of all types of individuals. The components of this should be particularly suited to youngsters who, for various reasons, have not learned well in the past. When this is accomplished the result is a different brand of education for learners who, for a multiplicity of reasons, have been classified as "under-achievers" or "slow learners." Actually, most so-called "slow learners" are not slow at all. They are simply students who have no commitment to learning.

What should the new *modus operandi* catering to non-committed learners be like? The new curricula must be far more yeasty than those of the past, engendering a much greater variety of educational programs. In addition to diversity, accommodation must be made for continuous academic mobility. Within this framework every student's program of studies can be one which suits his individual talents.

Varying the Curriculum

The Appropriate Placement school has a special commitment to youngsters who have not learned well in the past. The very nature of learning in an appropriate curriculum requires that the more challenging teaching positions relate to the learning problems of the more indifferent students. How is this accomplished? In gradeless education the able student has been freed from academic restraint and has proved that he can learn better when allowed to move ahead on his own. Studying independently, he no longer has to rely on recourse to teachers. He is able to spend many hours searching and learning on his own before commanding teacher attention. This releases talented teachers to generate new curricula for reluctant learners.

What are the factors which make the teaching of less able students more challenging in the nongraded school? (1) The textbook has been abandoned as ineffective; in its place the teacher is furnished with novel and provocative materials designed to jar and excite students' learning. (2) Teachers are encouraged to develop more materials through their own initiative. (3) The response of students who have been rejuvinated for learning by this new process provides abundant feelings of satisfaction to teachers who once were content only when teaching talented students. Confrontation with reluctant learners in a new setting and under favorable learning conditions makes a vast difference in the attitude of the more talented teachers. For the first time expert teachers cease demanding accelerated students. Instead, they are coming forward and saying, "Give me the ungifted and the unlearned for I am a professional and I can teach; the more difficult the student the better." This is not just a spasm response; the nongraded school has become another language. The intent is not just to ungrade students and the organization, but the teachers and the curriculum as well.

Linking the Curriculum to the Individual

The process of phasing students with similar backgrounds into programs of studies exclusively suited to their needs is especially effective with uncommitted learners. Through the system of phasing students into subjects, the appropriate placement plan with its change of pace and wide variety of curriculum experiences offers enormous appeal to this group of students. In effect, the development of phased learning, deliberately contrived for the individual and forged from the past performance and accomplishment of the school's students, has reshaped the curricula. The outline of the curricula resulting from this fusion is:

Achievement As Measured by Nationally Standardized Tests	Placement in the Curriculum
Performance between 1st and 20th percentile	Phase I [1]
Performance between 21st and 40th percentile	Phase II
Performance between 41st and 60th percentile	Phase III
Performance between 61st and 80th percentile	Phase IV
Performance between 81st and 90th percentile	Phase V

The new phased curricula for uncommitted learners, as for other students, are the outcome of a union between the individual's past performance and his future potential. It follows, then, that the individual student's program of studies is determined by his knowledge of a subject as measured by nationally standardized achievement tests. He is subsequently phased into the curricular situation most suitable to his individual requirements. From this point on the student's learning rate is set to a considerable degree by the group in which he finds himself. When he is able to maintain the pace of his

---

[1] It is the purpose of this chapter to deal only with the first and second phases of the curriculum. (A national application of achievement between the 1st and 40th percentile includes the nation's school dropouts which exceed 30% of all high school youth.)

classmates he acquires new confidence in his own ability. The emphasis is on building into each noncommitted learner a new capability for learning.

The New Physical Environment

Classes for non-committed learners come in all sizes. The size of each class is determined by three factors: (1) the ability of the youngsters; (2) the material to be presented; (3) the manner in which subject matter can be most effectively conveyed. The Appropriate Placement school is designed to free many teachers to teach small classes for students who have serious learning problems.

One of the earliest conclusions of the Appropriate Placement plan was that the conventional self-contained classroom is completely inappropriate for instructing students who, for various reasons, do not learn easily. Appropriateness of placement is committed to the notion that the average and the gifted student can be satisfactorily accommodated for learning in the ordinary classroom but unique facilities are essential if we are to awaken and kindle excitement in diffident learners. In order to encourage hesitant learners, classrooms must be carefully remodeled to reflect both comfort and pleasantness. The purpose of this is to convert commonplace classroom space into the more halcyon pattern of laboratory space. When students fail to learn in a classroom they must be given a new opportunity in a laboratory in which they can become more personally involved. The nongraded concept of a laboratory for reluctant learners has a number of emerging characteristics:

1. It must be air-conditioned in order to assure greater physical comfort for tense, frustrated students.
2. The floor should be carpeted for improved acoustical effects. (With reference to the latter, there are new rubber-like vinyl carpet products which give the desired atmosphere to the classroom. This material looks like

carpeting and when placed wall to wall gives amazingly satisfactory acoustical treatment.)

3. Color is important and decor makes a notable difference to apathetic students who have been carelessly educated through indifferent attention to their requirements.

The Concept of the Carrel

Another important dimension in the education of half-hearted learners is the degree of physical comfort transmitted by the furniture in which they are seated. Individualized carrels, previously described in detail, afford these students badly needed visual privacy, as well as secluded work space. While this is appropriate for all students, it is especially essential for classes involving reluctant learners. The carrel offers not only privacy and a wider work area as compared to the dreadfully uncomfortable chair-desk, but shelf space on which the student can keep equipment as well as books, paper and pencil, and other auxiliary learning materials. For example, in the reading laboratory every carrel can be furnished with a dictionary and a thesaurus for convenient use. In the mathematics laboratory, math puzzles, weighing devices, and objects of varying shapes and designs can be placed within easy reach of the student.

The introduction of a "relaxed element" into the learning environment as the result of increased physical comfort makes a great deal of difference to youngsters who do not learn easily. The improved work space supplied by carrels should be matched with chairs which are comfortable for sitting, but light for easy moving about. There are on the market light chairs which ideally suit this purpose.

The subject matter which is taught in the laboratory must be widely varied in content. The purpose of laboratory learning is twofold: (1) to awaken interest in the recalcitrant student;

TYPICAL LABORATORY DESIGN
FOR READING OR MATHEMATICS

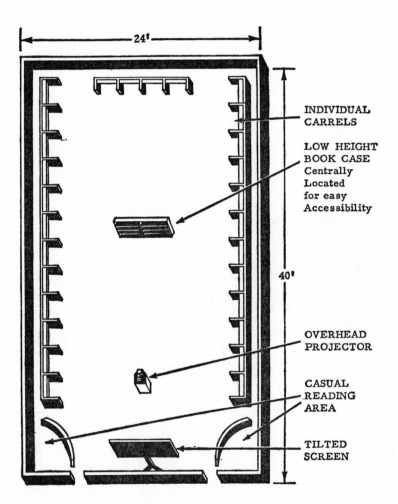

INDIVIDUAL
CARRELS

LOW HEIGHT
BOOK CASE
Centrally
Located
for easy
Accessibility

OVERHEAD
PROJECTOR

CASUAL
READING
AREA

TILTED
SCREEN

<u>FEATURES</u>
1. Air-conditioned For Comfort
2. 28 Wet Carrels W/Individual
   Electrical Outlets
3. Vinyl Rubber Carpet For
   Acoustical Advantages

163

*A DRY CARREL FUNCTIONS AS MOVEABLE FURNITURE
SINCE IT IS NOT WIRED FOR ELECTRICITY.

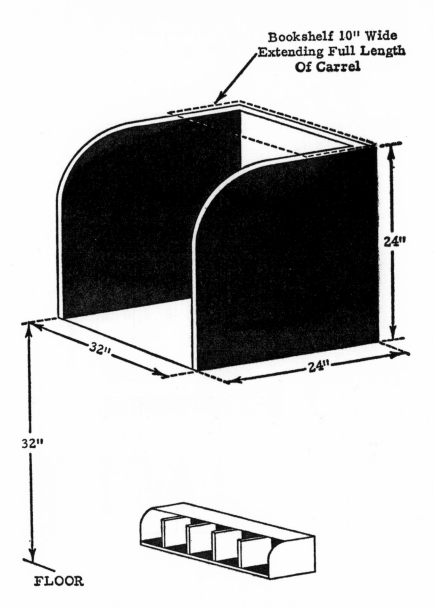

*WET CARREL DESIGN FOR INDIVIDUAL
AND MACHINE WORK IN READING

Bookshelf 10" Wide
Extending Full Length
Of Carrel

24"

32"

24"

32"

FLOOR

*WITH INDIVIDUAL ELECTRICAL RECEPTACLES

165

READING LABORATORY LEARNING CYCLE

	Round 1 LARGE GROUP ARRANGEMENT Brief Presentations Free & Directed Reading	Round 2 SPECIAL SEMINAR Phonics Instruction	Round 3 SPECIAL SEMINAR S.R.A. Accelerators Reading Machines Readers' Digest Skill Builders	Round 4 SPECIAL SEMINAR Discussion & Analysis
Monday	Groups A, B, 32 Students Disposed in Carrels	Group C 16 Students	Group D 16 Students	Group E 16 Students
Tuesday	Groups B, C, 32 Students Disposed in Carrels	Group D 16 Students	Group E 16 Students	Group A 16 Students
Wednesday	Groups C, D, 32 Students Disposed in Carrels	Group E 16 Students	Group A 16 Students	Group B 16 Students
Thursday	Groups D, E, 32 Students Disposed in Carrels	Group A 16 Students	Group B 16 Students	Group C 16 Students
Friday	Groups E, A, 32 Students Disposed in Carrels	Group B 16 Students	Group C 16 Students	Group D 16 Students

The English Laboratory, staffed by 4 teachers, is designed to accommodate the learning differences of 420 students.
Approximately 84 students are scheduled for laboratory involvement in a given period.
The number of students included in a particular round in the laboratory cycle is varied by increasing or decreasing the number of students in Round 1. The capacity of the large group arrangement is more responsive to stretching as learning in this area is centered around individual reading.

(2) to instill in him a new committment to learning. In the effort to do this, laboratory teachers must use a variety of unconventional approaches to learning. The laboratory must be an unorthodox place designed to rehabilitate the student with an undeveloped curiosity.

The Reading Laboratory

Reading is by far the most important subject in the curriculum. For this reason the learning of reading skills must take priority over all other learning. In the nongraded curriculum students who suffer from reading deficiencies should be scheduled out of conventional English classes and into a laboratory where they can receive intensive instruction in reading. The goals of the reading laboratory are:

1. To teach students mastery of minimal reading skills. The primary purpose is for students to learn how to attack and acquire new words in order to improve, comprehend and advance their basic knowledge of reading.
2. To provide instruction in the developmental aspects of reading. The intent is for basic readers to further improve their critical reading and to learn to read for aesthetic appreciation and pleasure. The objective is for students to become proficient with basic textbooks, auxiliary materials, and related library materials.

In addition to power instruction in reading, students in the nongraded reading laboratory should be assisted in the development of skills which condition them to become adept at dictionary use.

The Mathematics Laboratory

Next to reading, the most important subject in the curriculum is mathematics. The high priority given this subject is the contribution which it makes to the process of reasoning. What are the major components of a mathematics curriculum for non-committed learners? Addition, Subtraction, Multiplication, Division—these four operations should comprise the themes upon which the program for basic mathematics students must be centered.

In the conventional graded school, students who do not learn mathematics easily are relegated to a perfectly dreadful course called general mathematics. The traditional high school general mathematics course is a repetition of the same mathematics which the youngsters have been exposed to each year above the fourth grade. The result is that general mathematics at the high school level involves principles of mathematics which students did not learn in grades 5, 6, 7, 8, and 9 and it is taught again in their 10th year in the same old unimaginative way. As a consequence about all that students do in this course is to muddle through and satisfy the graduation requirement of a mathematics course offered at the high school level. In an appropriately designed school, students who have never achieved an understanding of the basic principles of mathematics are scheduled for a mathematics laboratory. To the student, the mathematics laboratory is a playroom where objects can be counted, moved, re-arranged, stacked, measured, joined or partitioned. It is a place where objects can be weighed and measured. Also, appropriate machines are at the student's disposal. It is a room full of pertinent books and a supply of writing tablets. The mathematics laboratory is full of mathematics study aids, this is where a student may learn the basic mathematics concepts which conventional classroom teaching prevented.

The History Laboratory

The plan of the history laboratory for uncommitted learners is vastly different from the reading and mathematics laboratories. The differences are physical as well as philosophical. Carrels which are so appropriate to the learning of reading and mathematics skills are not suitable for the history laboratory. Since the learning of history takes place best when students engage in discussion of historical issues, the most suitable furniture for the history laboratory is trapezodial tables. Trapezodial tables are formed so that students can be distributed to engage easily in discussion groups. Both furniture and students can be re-arranged for various sized group discussions.

Course content for students who are not motivated to learn history should evolve around courses in American and world affairs. These should not be current events courses, but, on the contrary, should strive to tie the major themes of modern historical trends to past history. A special emphasis in courses dealing in world and American affairs should be placed on the development of world peace. The students should be encouraged to see history in its wide, expansive dimension, rather than a fragmented collection of historical facts.

Science for Uncommitted Learners

In the area of science there are two very exciting curricula being developed which have enormous appeal for non-committed learners. One of these originated with the biological sciences curriculum study and is currently called "BSCS Special Materials for the Slow Learner." This special BSCS curriculum has taken the position that the basic aim of a course for un-committed learners is to develop in students the degree of scientific literacy which is needed by adults in a modern society. The structure of the BSCS course is based on the principle that laboratory work is the essence of learning in science for youngsters who are not well equipped with reading and mathematical skills. The differences between this special biology and the regular BSCS program lie in the fact that this special program does not go into detail as deeply as does the regular program. Furthermore, it affords more personal involvement through increased laboratory experiences. Another strength in the special materials lies in the fact that the reading assignments are uniquely designed for sophisticated interest but are very elementary in structure.

This new biology is structured around a novel approach. For example, student material is placed on individual sheets and punched for inclusion in a three-ring binder. Consequently, the student is able to construct his own textbook during the course as he writes up laboratory experiments and the results of class discussion. The significance of this lies in the fact that it is the first major study supported by the National Science Foundation which has involved itself with other than gifted students.

Time, Space, and Matter

Another notable development in the area of science for uncommitted learners is the Time, Space, and Matter course which is being developed at Princeton. While this new approach to science was originally developed for bright junior high school students, it is peculiarly suitable to uncommitted senior high school students.

The teaching strategy of Time, Space, and Matter comprises a sophisticated approach to the basic principles of science. The most striking characteristic of the course is the emphasis on active learning as contrasted with the traditional passivity of the learner. Throughout this interesting course the student is engaged in discovering things. He is constantly manipulating materials, making observations, carrying out investigations and interpreting the results. As a result of his deeply involved role in learning, the student frequently makes new discoveries. The result is a structured situation designed to optimize students' learning by discovery. In line with structured-discovery learning, the student is not presented with a textbook. Instead, he is given experiences from which he can build his own text. He records his own observations and arrives at his own conclusions which he revises and corrects, when necessary, in light of further investigations. The investigations posed for projects in Time, Space, and Matter both lead the student and involve him deeply in personalized learning.

Curriculum Strategy

The new appropriate placement curriculum should follow a mixed strategy—one that does not pretend to be highly planned and one which leaves room for "occasional" learning. Its design is deliberately planned to appeal not only to the senses of learning but to the instincts of imagination as well. The development of a variety of materials using the discovery approach precludes the need for the student to have constant resource to the teacher. The more deeply a student becomes involved in learning the greater is his commitment, shifting the responsibility of learning from the teacher to the student.

Emerging Techniques for Involving Uncommitted Learners

It is indeed unfortunate that we know so little about how youngsters learn. Uncommitted students have conditioned themselves against passive teaching approaches. Students, then, who do not learn easily must be placed in situations in which they are more personally involved: through their own discovery, and through small group discussion sessions.

Individual discovery most often takes place in the science laboratory, or through reading, either in the library or elsewhere. Small group discussions require even more skillful teaching. The following tips, developed by Pricilla Griffith of Melbourne High School, are especially helpful in provoking discussion among uncommitted learners.

Pointers for Effective Small Group Discussions

1. There are two criteria which a small group discussion topic must meet when it involves reluctant learners: (1) the students must be familiar with the topic; (2) it must be one about which students can generate feeling and controversy.

2. The teacher should rarely serve in the role of chairman. When he does he should develop skill at stating questions in a startling way.

3. The frequent use of parables or analogies on the proper level is effective. The aim is to create a visual perception of the issue.

4. One especially useful technique is to divide the class in half (if the subject warrants this treatment), then have half the class take one side of the question and the other the opposite side.

5. Assign roles to several members of the class, seeing that each student has a turn in each role. Roles which are effective are: questioner leader, criticizer-negative, criticizer-positive, and analyzer (summing up the discussion). This procedure works best when some of the first discussions involve informative discussions about the nature of these roles.

6. Another technique involves assigning a student a report on a topic he likes, which the other students then discuss. It cannot be a strictly informational topic, but one on which the reporter holds strong opinions and is, therefore, likely to make statements which spark discussion.

7. The discussion leader should have available a related topic to which he can switch if discussion bogs down, or a change-of-pace is needed.

8. The time for discussion should be scheduled in such a

way that it can be flexible; a half-hour when that is all that is needed. When the discussion has lessened in interest, students should return to other learning. Sessions should begin with half-hour periods and work up to one full class period as students become more adept at discussion skills.

The Importance of Placement

The appropriate placement school is concerned with the establishment of an educational system in which all students can be given the opportunity for the development and utilization of their individual abilities. Students must not be allowed to become discouraged with unfair competition and, after dropping out of school, become social problems because they are unable to hold jobs due to their lack of basic education. Through the concentrated efforts of competent teachers, an imaginative program can be brought into being which not only assists the student to remedy deficiencies in his education but which places him in a high school situation where he is truly accepted.

Conclusion

There can be no final summing up of the program in a nongraded school for there is never a time when conditions are static. There is constant change as teachers become aware of new concepts within their subject areas and try newly discovered ideas to reinforce existing teaching techniques. There is an aura of adventure as whole new departments are created to fit the burgeoning needs of students. New concepts of education automatically replace old ones, as students, parents, and teachers become aware of the validity of new ideas and thrust aside archaic patterns and standards. The story of the nongraded school this year will not be the story of the nongraded school next year, because as soon as a program is working well there is always the challenge to improve it, to refine it, to make it obsolete.

The time has come when we must examine and appraise our entire educational system, recognizing candidly those areas in which it has failed and dedicating ourselves to its improvement. Only if we do this may we look forward to a day when learning will have regained both the stature and the excitement it so rightly deserves in a society such as ours. First steps are always difficult, though, and may be painful as well. Schools embarking on a program of change, seeking to improve and to fulfill better the trust invested in them, may find themselves isolated from their neighbors. Innovators always seem out of step with their more conventional contemporaries. But, if we believe in ourselves and in the vital importance of the challenge before us, it is the Appropriate Placement school that will be setting the new pace.

APPENDIX

One of the best articles ever written about nongraded schools is by a parent. In presenting the article, entitled *A Parent's Blueprint,* I feel compelled to say something about the status of school administration. Many administrators seem to be unaware of either the magnitude or the acceleration of the extravagant changes which are taking place in society. This sounds like a devastating indictment of my profession, but it must be admitted that all too often, when school administrators are confronted with awesome problems, they have a distressing tendency to bury their heads in the sand. Furthermore, administrators often demur when faced with heady and unusual ideas. They think that they can bring about change by tiptoeing around to state and national meetings. There are two ways to get to the top of an oak tree. One is to climb it, the other is to sit on an acorn. Conventional school administrators have chosen to sit.

It appears to me that unless school administrators seize the initiative and champion ideas of change and progress, the prerogative of leadership will soon be taken from them. We must have change regardless of how sturdily conventional administrators resist. Unless we manage to pace educational change to social change, there will be a great retreat along the educational front. Its consequence will be a complete surrender of educational leadership.

The top administrative positions in the nation's schools should no longer be filled by individuals who have had numerous courses in school administration. The superintendency should be based on training in executive management and leadership precisely as top executive posts are filled in government and industry. The superintendent has no contact with children and very little contact with teachers—his job is management. Unless executive management techniques are used in the training of superintendents, the generals of education will never become leaders in social renewal and educational revolution. But, what does a parent have to say?

A Parent's Blueprint [1]

For twelve years I have watched public education deteriorate. My criticisms have been resented as unwarranted lay interference in professional matters and my questions have been countered with that stock answer reserved for all busybodies: "Just how would you do it?"

Today I am answering that challenge. As a parent with twenty-three child-school-years behind me, I, along with millions of other parents, have earned the right to speak as a "professional" layman. "Professional layman" may sound like an amusing anomaly to some, but most parents will acknowl-

---

[1] Garrett, Mildred B., "A Parent's Blueprint," *Saturday Review*, p. 55, December 17, 1960.

edge the humor with a wry smile as they go on proving they are not amateurs.

We professional laymen have gone through a long and exacting course of study, not on a college campus, but on the school grounds. Our lectures have been in such meetings as PTA, mental health, and child study groups. Our discussions have ranged from formal panels to impromptu grocery-store sessions. Our labs, sometimes long and arduous, have been held in our homes and in our schools. Our texts have been our own children's school books and our outside reading has consisted of everything on education in the library and the public press. We have even had examinations—some of them searching and unexpected! They have assumed unorthodox forms but nevertheless demanded quick decisions and the right answers. They have included everything from a demand for "something about compost heaps with a lot of pictures" from one of the children to an urgent summons from the principal.

We laymen know that support of public education involves more than enrolling our children in school, working in the PTA, and voting in Board of Education and bond issue elections, but we have meekly refrained from assuming any responsibility for what goes on in the classroom because we have allowed ourselves to be deluded by impressive statistics, intimidated by experts, and lulled by easy catch phrases. As a result we have lost confidence in our ability to function as intelligent citizens and competent parents and, through our own stupidity, fear, and inertia, have lost control of our schools.

I am accepting the challenge to describe the kind of schools I would like with the fervent hope that other laymen will also speak up and tell in public what they have been telling so well in private over the grocery carts and coffee cups: the kind of education they would like for their children.

We have already had too much lay educator controversy.

Such quarreling has resulted in nothing but bitterness and recrimination. I have no desire to continue such pointless arguments, nor am I willing or competent to cite educational research, statistics, or authorities. The conclusions I have reached and the changes I advocate have all grown slowly, and sometimes painfully, out of my "professional" education.

I believe we are in a position to have better schools now than would have been possible even a decade ago. Our educators have tabulated and organized a great store of valuable knowledge about child growth and the learning processes. They have recognized the importance of "the whole child" but accepted the fact of individual differences. The community has undertaken the responsibility for the education of all children in areas beyond the three Rs. Teachers colleges have improved the quality of their training, and certification requirements for teachers have been raised along with their salaries.

All of these things are prime ingredients for good schools— but have we used them wisely? In our eagerness to free our children from the narrow confines and harmful practices of the little red schoolhouse, have we also destroyed the heart of public education? Have we accepted these new theories, concepts, practices, and services so enthusiastically that we have allowed them to become dangerous masters forcing us to bypass the real purpose of our schools?

The time has come to specify the purpose of our schools in order to establish a fixed point of reference from which we can view the whole situation while we reorient our thinking and planning. A few years ago the emphasis was on full personality development. Before that it was on vocational training or social adjustment. Today our schools are being pressured into another rush of frenzied activity by our national need for more scientists and engineers. Frantic demands are being made to find the bright child, segregate him, and teach him all he can learn in mathematics and science. Unless we call a halt, something else is certain to follow after this emergency is over. No nation can long survive such educational folly as that which we are pursuing by concentrating all our effort on one group of children and one segment of the curriculum today and on another tomorrow.

"The aims of education" and "the purpose of the schools" are not synonymous terms. Let us recognize the "aims of education" as being the maximum development of "the whole child" but accept the fact that only the whole community can educate the whole child. This will narrow the purpose of the school to the specific sphere of responsibility which has been established by tradition—academic training and intellectual development—academic training meaning transmission of the culture of mankind and intellectual development meaning the creative use of that knowledge.

I believe that deliberately limiting the purpose of the schools will contribute much to the development of "the whole child." We will see our children not only acquiring disciplined minds and broader intellectual interests but enriched spirits and educated hearts as well. To say that education is "of the mind" does not imply denial or neglect of other aspects of child growth. By specifying the "mind" we are only defining the avenue of approach the school will take in assuming its share of the responsibility for the education of the whole child.

We cannot operate our new single-purpose, individual-centered school under the traditional vertical grade system. This system uses the most unreliable of all criteria—chronological age—as the basis for a child's progress through the school. Teachers know this and are trying every sort of makeshift to minimize the harm: achievement level groups within each classroom, reading clinics, remedial arithmetic teams, social promotion, and so on. They are complicating relatively simple concepts and practices by trying to fit them into an unrealistic and inefficient organization of rigid grades cut into illogical segments called elementary, junior high, and senior high. In our new schools we will sweep away these relics of the past and organize a new system to fit our new needs.

We will establish three four-year blocks of instruction time: primary, intermediate and senior. The "four-year" time element will have little meaning, however, since the actual time spent in any unit by a child will depend on his individual achievement and may vary from three to five years. Time will never be an important element in meeting standards but is a necessary factor in establishing them. Achievement requirements will be so devised that they can be met in the allotted time by the average child with consistent effort under good instruction. Minimum requirements will be in effect only for the child of very low capacity.

Movement will be forward from level to level as each child proves himself ready for more advanced work. Such a fluid structure will not only adapt itself to the basic differences in capacity but will also provide for changes in each child's rhythm of learning. Every child will have the opportunity to compensate for his inevitable periods of diminished efficiency by being allowed to take full advantage of his periods of peak achievement. Rigid requirements within a flexible time schedule will replace the current system of flexible requirements within a rigid time schedule.

The emphasis on individual differences in mental power in no way minimizes the importance of the child's spiritual, emotional, social, and physical development. Differences in these spheres will be recognized and used as powerful factors in promoting intellectual growth. At the same time, the cultivation of the child's mind will be the means by which the school discharges its share of the responsibility toward the unfolding of each complicated, mysterious, and sacred personality that is "the whole child." Trained leadership will be needed to implement this policy and this will require changes in teacher preparation.

Since the ungraded school is organized for the express purpose of more efficiently caring for individual differences, some valid means of arriving at these differences must be established. Fortunately, standardized group and individual tests are available to measure, with varying degrees of accuracy, all phases of child growth. Our schools will use them all, but with full knowledge of their limitations. They will be the valuable tools they were designed to be because all the mumbo-jumbo that now surrounds them will be swept away. Having lost their awesome and mysterious powers, they can be used for what they are: limited mechanical devices that point the way for further joint exploration by counselors, teachers, and parents.

The same organization and methods designed to care for individual differences will also provide for the equally important likenesses of individuals—those associations built on congenialities of taste, interest, and talent, and the companionships possible within common stages of maturity. Since each school operates as a unit, with constant reshuffling taking place within its academic organization, there will be no rigid level demarcations to act as artificial barriers to the natural attraction of like to like. No child will be frozen in any arbitrary group, but will be free to seek the companionships that fulfill his current needs.

This freedom from the imposed conformity of the chronological grade system is particularly important in the intermediate and senior units for these are the years of unpredictable divergencies and inequalities for many, and admittedly difficult years for parents and teachers. Even so, we will remember that adolescence is only one stage in the democratic process of growing up and does not warrant the concentrated attention that has been lavished on it during the last two decades. We have isolated the "teenagers" in an artificial and unrealistic environment and have treated them as though they were an unusual and precious segment of human kind. They are not: they are individuals like the rest of us.

We laymen are pretty well agreed that the situation is getting out of hand. Because we know that it is the physical and sexual changes that trigger most of the manifestations of adolescence we enthusiastically promote premature boy-girl relationships with all their social complications and dangers. We interpret our adolescent's vague yearnings for independence as a need for immediate freedom and give them drivers' licenses and dating privileges. We see their boisterous behavior as manifestations of the insecurity born of erratic emotional responses and condone bad manners. We acknowledge their longing for wider horizons by exposing them to vocational "exploratory" courses. We even provide for their sharp fluctuations in energy by reducing over-all academic requirements so as not to overburden them, yet seek year-round extracurricular and recreational activities to keep them busy! What we have succeeded in doing—parents, educators, psychologists, and sociologists together—has been to create that mythical kind of human being we call the "teenager."

The new ungraded intermediate and senior units will provide the flexibility necessary to allow the pre-adolescent or adolescent to develop intellectually as fast as he can without prolonging a false childhood or enforcing a premature adulthood. Each can satisfy his recurrent and compelling needs and interests, be they childish or mature. We shall be aware of the adolescent's special problems, of course, but we shall be relaxed about them. We shall counter his demands for independence by demands of our own that he earn his freedom. We shall refuse to be victims of his emotional turmoil but shall show him how his insecurity can be conquered by the satisfactions that come from a hard job well done. Most important of all, we shall stop analyzing him and hovering over him: instead, we shall step aside long enough to give him the time and space in which to grow.

Our new schools will no more assume that all adolescents are bewildered and unhappy because they are living through a period of change than that all first-graders have a stomachache because they are living through a period subject to intestinal upsets.

The curriculum will be the same for all. Only the pace and range will be varied to conform to the demands of each level.

No lines will be drawn between the college-bound and the job-bound student; there will be no assumption that the job-seeking student will have less need of mathematics, science, history, government, literature, language and the arts than his college-bound brother. There will be no betrayal of the individual by setting apart one group of children and offering them vocational training with only the bare bones of literature, history, and the arts because they are not "college material" or "college-bound."

Some students will plod along and some will race ahead but each will, on graduation, have a broad understanding of the world about him, a comprehensive knowledge of his past, a lasting appreciation of his heritage, and a satisfying capacity for communicating with his fellows, all of which will contribute to his realization of the present and the creation of his future.

The means used by the school to translate its purpose into its goals is the curriculum. In our uncomplicated way of thinking, we laymen believe that the curriculum should be exactly what the dictionary says it is: "a specified course of study." We think of the ideal curriculum as a foundation blueprint that specifies the laying of each stone in its logical sequence. We are aware that "logical sequence" involves more than the continuity inherent in the subject itself and must also include the growth, development, and learning process of the individual child. Curriculum design is a complicated process, the actual drawing of which must be in the hands of teachers. First, however, they must have a clear mandate from the community as to the purpose for which it maintains its schools and the ultimate goals it seeks.

All the planning in the world cannot make a good school—only good teachers can do that—and we laymen have never been convinced that "fully certified" teachers are necessarily good teachers. Being laymen, however, we are fully aware of and deeply concerned about the individual teacher's performance in the classroom as measured by the quality of the learning that takes place there. We fear that mediocrity will remain permanently entrenched so long as we maintain our present policies of across-the-board pay raises and tenure rights, coupled with total disregard for standards of performance.

In our new schools we shall classify and pay teachers on the basis of their achievement in the classroom instead of their degrees and length of service. The argument against incentive pay has been that there is no equitable way of evaluating a teacher's performance in the classroom. Such contentions have a certain validity in the present confused state of public education, where trying to evaluate anything is like trying to take tuck in a cloud. The goal of educating "the whole child" is hardly something to be pinned down, much less evaluated.

Our new schools, organized as they are to operate within the limits of a stated purpose toward a predetermined goal with established standards and a defined curriculum, can evaluate the intellectual growth and academic achievement of their pupils. In the laymen's mind it is obvious that any tests and techniques that can appraise the extent and quality of the learning must automatically appraise the extent and quality of the teaching.

Minimum salaries will be established for all teachers, but

what each makes after the probationary period will be based on her worth as reflected by the progress of her pupils. The highest salaries paid will be comparable to the incomes of other top professional people. A program of selective recruiting, rigorous training, and strict classification combined with commensurate rewards will put teachers worthy of our children into the classrooms—men and women who are more than members of a respected profession but are a fellowship dedicated to making our children stretch their minds, open their hearts, and try their wings.

The whole program will be wasted, however, unless we also provide an environment in which teachers can make full use of their training and talents. Our new schools will start by freeing them from the two most obvious burdens: administrative domination and interference, and non-teaching chores. We will no longer need a complicated administrative organization; in our schools educational policies and practices will originate at the top, which is the classroom.

Since many time-wasting chores are part of classroom activity, each teacher will have an aide to assist her. New certification requirements will provide for a corps of subprofessionals to fill these positions, which, if necessary, can be supplemented by competent lay people, some of whom may work on a part-time basis.

In order to regain control of their schools, citizens must first spend long hours of earnest consultation together, without the benefit of professional advice, to arrive at common educational needs and aspirations from which they can develop specific purposes and goals. Not until these purposes and goals are written in language that all can understand will the community seek professional guidance. Then the long period of cooperative evaluation and planning will begin. Every educational philosophy and practice and every idea and plan advanced by both laymen and teachers will be subjected to one final test: "Is it in line with our stated purpose and will it advance us toward our specified goals?"

Thus, by establishing its own criteria, the community will not only free itself from the "Cult of the Sacred Average" with its deification of the "National Norm," but will also be able to think beyond "minimum requirements" as dictated by college entrance requirements and state accreditation. Here, at last, will be a clearly defined framework within which the possibility for bold and creative planning are unlimited. The only inhibiting factors will be those inherent in the planners themselves: a nostalgic longing for the past, a stubborn insistence on the sanctity of tradition, blind reliance on the virtues of custom, and a credulous belief in the infallibility of any educational research, authority, or school of thought.

Financial support will be no problem in the community whose citizens control their schools and actively participate in the education of their children, for they will be buying exactly what they want and will be in a position to know whether they are getting full value for their money. We laymen have always known that shoddy education was no bargain even at greatly reduced rates and have been willing to pay any price for the best. If we have appeared niggardly in the past it was because we suspected that we were not getting all that we thought we were buying.

This description of the kind of schools that I wish my children could have attended is only one answer to a nationwide challenge. Not until laymen in every school district from Maine to California answer the same challenge will local control of our schools be a reality or public education be a success in terms of either personal fulfillment or national security.

Whether you, as a layman, have the benefit of one or fifty child-school-years experience, you are obligated to make some answer to the challenge by the simple fact that you are a parent and a contributing member of our society. The knowledge and skills that you use every day in your home and your work, plus what you know about your child and his playmates, makes you a competent observer.

We are moving out of the era of the well-adjusted illiterate and, unless we act promptly, straight into the era of the scientific illiterate. Only bold planning and positive action by the professional laymen of each community can prevent the same old mistakes from being made all over again.

INDEX

INDEX